NORWEGIAN

PHRASEBOOK & DICTIONARY

Contacting the Editors

Every effort has been made to provide accurate information in this publication, but changes are inevitable. The publisher cannot be responsible for any resulting loss, inconvenience or injury. We would appreciate it if readers would call our attention to any errors or outdated information. We also welcome your suggestions; if you come across a relevant expression not in our phrase book, please contact us at: **hello@insightguides.com**

All Rights Reserved
© 2016 Apa Digital (CH) AG and Apa Publications (UK) Ltd.

First Edition: 2016
Printed in China

Cover & Interior Design: Pawel Pasternak
Production: AM Services
Production Manager: Vicky Glover
Cover Photo: Shutterstock

Interior Photos: Shutterstock

CONTENTS

INTRODUCTION

GETTING STARTED

EXPLORING

ACTIVITIES

HEALTH & SAFETY

FOOD & DRINK

GOING OUT

DICTIONARY

PRONUNCIATION

This section is designed to make you familiar with the sounds of Norwegian by using our simplified phonetic transcription. You'll find the pronunciation of the Norwegian letters explained below, together with their 'imitated' equivalents (the Norwegian alphabet is the same as in English, with the addition of the letters æ, ø and å). This phonetic system is used throughout the phrase book; simply read the pronunciation as if it were English, noting any special rules below.

Stress has been indicated in the phonetic transcription with underlining, tone with the accent marks and long vowels with bold.

CONSONANTS

Letter	Approximate Pronunciation	Symbol	Example	Pronunciation
g	1. before i and y, (sometimes before ei) like y in yes	y	gi	y**ee**
	2. elsewhere, like g in go	g	gått	goht
gj	like y in yes	y	gjest	yehst
j	like y in yes	y	ja	yah
k	1. before i, y and ei like h in hue, but with the tongue raised a little higher	kh	kino	<u>kh**ee**</u> • nu
	2. elsewhere, like k in kit	k	kaffe	<u>kahf´</u> • fuh
kj	like h in hue, but with the tongue raised a little higher	kh	kjøre	<u>kh**ur**ˋ</u> • ruh
r	rolled near the front of the mouth	r	rare	<u>rahˋ</u> • ruh

Letter	Approximate Pronunciation	Symbol	Example	Pronunciation
s	like s in sit	s	spise	*sp**ee**` • suh*
sj	like sh in shut	sh	stasjon	*stah • sh**oo**´n*
sk	1. before i and y (sometimes before øy), like sh in shut	sh	ski	*sh**ee***
	2. elsewhere, like sk in skate	sk	skole	*sk**oo**` • luh*
skj	like sh in shut	sh	skje	*sh**eh***
w	like v in vice	v	whisky	*v**ih**s´ • kih*
z	like s in sit	s	zoom	*s**oo**m*

Letters b, c, d, f, h, l, m, n, p, q, t, v, x are generally pronounced as in English.

VOWELS

Letter	Approximate Pronunciation	Symbol	Example	Pronunciation
a	1. like a in father, but longer	ah	tak	*tahk*
	2. like a in father	ah	takk	*tahk*
e	1. like e in get, but longer	eh	sent	*sehnt*
	2. like e in get	eh	penn	*pehn*
	3. like a in bad	a	her	*har*
	4. before r, like a in bad	a	herre	*ha` • ruh*
	5. like u in uncle	uh	sitte	*s**ih**` • tuh*
i	1. like ee in bee	ee	hit	*heet*
	2. like i in sit	ih	sitt	*siht*

Letter	Approximate Pronunciation	Symbol	Example	Pronunciation
o	1. like oo in soon, with lips tightly rounded	oo	ord	*oor*
	2. like aw in saw	aw	tog	*tawg*
	3. like u in put, with lips tightly rounded	u	ost	*ust*
	4. like o in cloth	oh	stoppe	<u>*stohp*</u>` • *puh*
	5. before r, like oo in soon	oo	hvor	*voor*
u	1. like ew in few, but longer	ew	mur	*mewr*
	2. like ew in few	ew	busk	*bewsk*
	3. like u in put, with lips tightly rounded	u	bukk	*buk*
y	1. like ui in fruit, but longer	ui	myr	*muir*
	2. like ui in fruit	ui	bygge	<u>*buig*</u>` • *guh*
æ	1. like a in bad, but longer	a	lære	<u>*la*</u>` • *ruh*
	2. like a in bad	a	færre	<u>*far*</u>´ • *ruh*
ø	1. like ur in fur, but longer and with lips rounded	ur	blø	*blur*
	2. like ur in fur, with lips rounded	ur	sønn	*surn*
å	1. like aw in saw, but longer	aw	såpe	<u>*saw*</u>` • *puh*
	2. like o in cloth	oh	gått	*goht*

VOWELS COMBINATIONS

Letter	Approximate Pronunciation	Symbol	Example	Pronunciation
ai	like ie in tie	**ie**	**mais**	*mies*
au	like ev in ever	**ev**	**sau**	*sev*
ei	like ay in say	**ay**	**geit**	*yayt*
eg	at the end of a word and before n, like ay in say	**ay**	**jeg**	*yay*
oi	like oi in oil	**oi**	**koie**	*koi` • uh*
øy	like ur + y	**ury**	**høy**	*hury*

(i)

In Norwegian, vowel length distinguishes meaning. All vowels come in two lengths, long and short. Long vowels are in bold throughout the phonetics.

Norwegian is a tonal language. This means that tone is used to distinguish between certain words, which otherwise would sound the same. For example:

hender (*hehn´ • nuhr*), tone 1 = plural of **hånd** (hand)
hender (*hehn` • nuhr*), tone 2 = present tense of **hende** (happen)

In the phonetics, tone 1, which is a rising tone (i.e., starts low and rises in pitch) is marked with the acute accent (´); tone 2, which is a falling tone (i.e., starts high and lowers in pitch), with the grave accent (`).

In Norwegian, consonants are silent in the following situations:

1. The letter **d** is generally silent after **l**, **n** or **r** (e.g. **holde**, **land**, **gård**), and sometimes at the end of words (e.g. **god**, **med**).
2. The letter **g** is silent in the endings **-lig** and **-ig**.
3. The letter **h** is silent when followed by a consonant (e.g. **hjem**, **hva**).
4. The letter **t** is silent in the definite form ('the') of neuter nouns (e.g., **eplet**) and in the pronoun **det**.
5. The letter **v** is silent in certain words (e.g. **selv**, **tolv**, **halv**).
6. In the eastern part of Norway the letter **r** is silent when followed by **l**, **n**, **s**, **t** (and sometimes **d**). These consonants are pronounced with the tip of the tongue turned up well behind the front teeth. The **r** then ceases to be pronounced, but influences the tone of the following consonant. This 'retroflex' pronunciation also occurs in words ending with an **r** if the following word begins with a **d**, **l**, **n**, **s** or **t**.

HOW TO USE THE APP

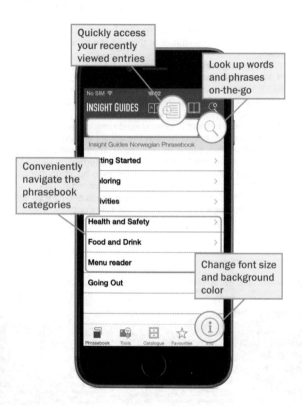

Quickly access your recently viewed entries

Look up words and phrases on-the-go

Conveniently navigate the phrasebook categories

Change font size and background color

Save the most useful everyday words and phrases to your Favorites

Use the Flash Cards Quiz to learn and memorize new words easily

Take all digital advantages of the app: listen to words and phrases pronounced by native speakers

No SIM 📶   18:16

Insight Guides Norwegian Phrasebook

Is there a traditional Norwegian/ an inexpensive restaurant near here?

Fins det en typisk norsk/billig restaurant i nærheten?

fihns deh ehn <u>tui</u>´•pihsk nohrsk/ bihl`•lih rehs•tew•<u>rahng</u>´ ih <u>nar</u>´•heh•tuhn

Can you reco...   A table for......

Phrasebook   Tools   Catalogue   Favourites   Info

To learn how to activate the app, see the inside back cover of this phrasebook.

GRAMMAR

Norway has two official written, mutually comprehensible languages, **bokmål** and **nynorsk**. **Bokmål** is the most common and is used throughout this book although a traveler in Norway should expect to come across both.

VERBS

The present tense of regular verbs in Norwegian is formed by adding **-er** to the stem of the verb. The past tense is formed by **-et** or **-te**. The future is formed with **skal** or **vil** + infinitive. This applies to all persons (e.g., I, you, he, she, it, etc.). Following are the present, past and future forms of the verbs **å bytte** (to change) and **å kjøpe** (to buy).

	PRESENT	PAST	FUTURE
å bytte (to change)	bytter	byttet	skal/vil bytte
å kjøpe (to buy)	kjøper	kjøpte	skal/vil kjøpe

IRREGULAR VERBS

There are a number of irregular verbs in Norwegian; these must be memorized. Like regular verbs, however, the irregular verb form remains the same, irrespective of person(s). Following are the present, past and future conjugations for a few important, useful irregular verbs.

	PRESENT	PAST	FUTURE
å være (to be)	**er**	**var**	**skal/vil være**
å ha (to have)	**har**	**hadde**	**skal/vil ha**
å kunne (to be able to, can)	**kan**	**kunne**	**skal/vil kunne**
å spørre (to ask)	**spør**	**spurte**	**skal/vil spørre**

IMPERATIVES

The imperative is generally the same form as the stem of the verb:

Examples:

Bytt! Change!   **Kjøp!** Buy!   **Gå!** Go!

NOUNS

Nouns in Norwegian can be common (masculine/feminine), feminine or neuter. There are no easy rules for determining the gender. It is best to learn each new word with its accompanying article.

The plural of most nouns is formed by an **-(e)r** ending (indefinite plural) or an **-(e)ne** ending (definite plural).

Examples:

common:	**biler**	cars	**bilene**	the cars
neuter:	**epler**	apples	**eplene**	the apples

Many monosyllabic nouns have irregular plurals:

en mann	a man	**menn**	men	**mennene**	the men
en sko	a shoe	**sko**	shoes	**skoene**	the shoes
et hus	a house	**hus**	houses	**husene**	the houses
et barn	a child	**barn**	children	**barna**	the children

Possession is shown by adding **-s** (singular and plural). Note that there is no apostrophe.

Examples:
Johns bror	John's brother
hotellets eier	the owner of the hotel
barnas far	the children's father

ARTICLES

The article (a, an, the) shows the gender of a Norwegian noun, which can be common (masculine/feminine), feminine or neuter. Note that the majority of feminine nouns also have a common form, but usually appear in their feminine form.

1. Indefinite article (a/an)
common:	**en bil**	a car
feminine:	**en** (*or* **ei**) **jente**	a girl
neuter:	**et eple**	an apple

2. Definite article (the)
Where in English one says 'the house', Norwegians tag the definite article onto the end of the noun and say 'house-the'. In common nouns 'the' is **-(e)n**, in feminine nouns, **a** and in neuter nouns, **-(e)t**.

Examples:
common:	**bilen**	the car
feminine:	**jenta**	the girl
neuter:	**eplet**	the apple

PERSONAL PRONOUNS

I	**jeg**
you	**du**
he	**han**
she	**hun**
it	**den/det**
we	**vi**

you (plural)   **dere**
they   **de**

The two forms for 'it' refer to the gender. **Den** refers to masculine and feminine nouns, **det** to neuter nouns.
Norwegian has two forms for 'you': **du** (informal) and **De** (formal). However, today, the use of the formal **De** has practically disappeared from the language.

NEGATION

Negation is expressed by using the adverb **ikke** (not). It is usually placed immediately after the verb in a main clause. In compound tenses, **ikke** appears between the auxiliary and the main verb.

Jeg snakker norsk.   I speak Norwegian.
Jeg snakker ikke norsk.   I do not speak Norwegian.

QUESTIONS

Questions are generally formed by reversing the order of the subject and the verb:

Examples:
Bussen stanser her.   The bus stops here.
Stanser bussen her?   Does the bus stop here?
Jeg kommer i kveld.   I am coming tonight.
Kommer du i kveld?   Are you coming tonight?

ADJECTIVES

An adjective agrees with the noun it modifies in gender and number. For the indefinite form, the neuter is generally formed by adding **-t**, the plural by adding **-e**.

Examples:

(en) stor hund	(a) big dog	**store hunder**	big dogs
(et) stort hus	(a) big house	**store hus**	big houses

For the definite form of the adjective, add the ending **-e** (common, neuter and plural). This form is used when the adjective is preceded by **den, det, de** (the definite article used with adjectives) or by a demonstrative or a possessive adjective.

Examples:

den store hunden	the big dog
de store hundene	the big dogs
det store huset	the big house
de store husene	the big houses

COMPARATIVE & SUPERLATIVE

The comparative and superlative are normally formed either by adding the ending **-(e)re** and **-(e)st**, respectively, to the adjective, or by putting **mer** (more) and **mest** (most) before the adjective.

Examples:

stor/større/størst	big/bigger/biggest
lett/lettere/lettest	easy/easier/easiest
imponerende/mer imponerende/	impressive/more impressive/
mest imponerende	the most impressive

DEMONSTRATIVE ADJECTIVES

A demonstrative adjective agrees with the noun it modifies in gender and number. If it doesn't refer to a noun, the neuter form is used, e.g., **Hva er det?** What is that?

	COMMON	NEUTER	PLURAL
this/these	**denne**	**dette**	**disse**
that/those	**den**	**det**	**de**

ADVERBS

Adverbs are often formed by adding **-t** to the corresponding adjective.

rask/raskt	quick/quickly
langsom/langsomt	slow/slowly

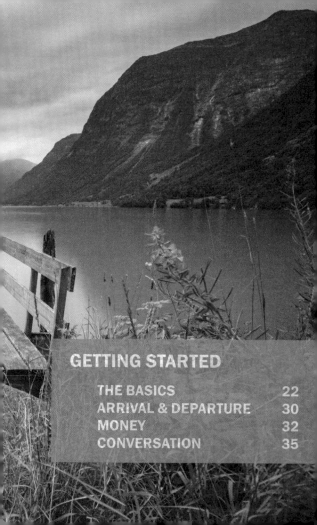

GETTING STARTED

THE BASICS

NUMBERS

NEED TO KNOW

0	**null**	*newl*
1	**en**	*ehn*
2	**to**	*too*
3	**tre**	*treh*
4	**fire**	*fee`•ruh*
5	**fem**	*fehm*
6	**seks**	*sehks*
7	**sju**	*shew*
8	**åtte**	*oht`•tuh*
9	**ni**	*nee*
10	**ti**	*tee*
11	**elleve**	*ehl`•vuh*
12	**tolv**	*tohl*

13	**tretten**
	treh`t • _tuhn_
14	**fjorten**
	fyu` • _rtuhn_
15	**femten**
	fehm` • _tuhn_
16	**seksten**
	says` • _tuhn_
17	**sytten**
	surt` • _tuhn_
18	**atten**
	aht` • _tuhn_
19	**nitten**
	niht` • _tuhn_
20	**tjue**
	khew` • _uh_
21	**tjueen**
	khew • _uh_ • **_eh´n_**
22	**tjueto**
	khew • _uh_ • **_too´_**
30	**tretti**
	treht´ • _tih_
31	**trettien**
	treht • _tih_ • **_eh´n_**
40	**førti**
	furr´ • _tih_
50	**femti**
	fehm´ • _tih_
60	**seksti**
	sehks´ • _tih_
70	**sytti**
	surt´ • _tih_

90	**nitti**
	niht´ • tih
100	**hundre**
	hewn` • druh
101	**hundreogen**
	hewn • druh • oh • _eh´n_
200	**to hundre**
	too _hewn_` • druh
500	**fem hundre**
	fehm _hewn_` • druh
1,000	**tusen**
	tew´ • suhn
10,000	**ti tusen**
	tee _tew´_ • suhn
1,000,000	**en million**
	ehn mihl • _yoo´n_

ORDINAL NUMBERS

first	**første**
	furr` • stuh
second	**andre**
	ahn` • druh
third	**tredje**
	trehd` • yuh
fourth	**fjerde**
	fya` • ruh
fifth	**femte**
	fehm` • tuh
once	**en gang**
	ehn gahng
twice	**to ganger**
	too _gahng_` • uhr
three times	**tre ganger**
	treh _gahng_` • uhr

TIME

NEED TO KNOW

What time is it?	**Hvor mye er klokken?**
	voor mui ` • uh ar klohk ` • kuhn
It's noon [midday].	**Den er tolv.**
	dehn ar tohl
At midnight.	**Ved midnatt.**
	veh mihd ´ • naht
From nine o'clock to five o'clock.	**Fra klokken ni til klokken fem.**
	fra klohk ` • kuhn nee tihl klohk ` • kuhn fehm
Twenty after [past] four.	**Ti på halv fem.**
	tee poh hahl fehm
A quarter to nine.	**Kvart på ni.**
	kvahrt poh nee
5:30 a.m./p.m.	**Fem tretti/Sytten tretti.**
	fehm treht ´ • tih/surt ` • tuhn treht ´ • tih
Half past five.	**Halv seks.**
	hahl sehks

DAYS

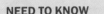

NEED TO KNOW

Monday	**mandag**
	mahn´ • dahg
Tuesday	**tirsdag**
	teers´ • dahg
Wednesday	**onsdag**
	uns´ • dahg
Thursday	**torsdag**
	tawrs´ • dahg
Friday	**fredag**
	freh´ • dahg
Saturday	**lørdag**
	lurr´ • dahg
Sunday	**søndag**
	surn´ • dahg

DATES

yesterday	**i går**
	ih gawr
today	**i dag**
	ih dahg
tomorrow	**i morgen**
	ih mawr` • uhn
day	**dag**
	dahg
week	**uke**
	_ew`_ • kuh
month	**måned**
	maw` • nuhd

year	**år**
	awr

MONTHS

January	**januar**
	yah • new • __ah ´__ r
February	**februar**
	feh • brew • __ah ´__ r
March	**mars**
	mahrs
April	**april**
	ahp • __ree ´__ l
May	**mai**
	mie
June	**juni**
	__yew ´__ • nee
July	**juli**
	__yew ´__ • lee
August	**august**
	ev • __gews ´__ t
September	**september**
	sehp • __tehm ´__ • buhr

October	**oktober**	
	ohk • taw´ • buhr	
November	**november**	
	nu • vehm´ • buhr	
December	**desember**	
	deh • sehm´ • buhr	

SEASONS

spring	**vår**
	vawr
summer	**sommer**
	sohm` • muhr
fall [autumn]	**høst**
	hurst
winter	**vinter**
	vihn´ • tuhr

Major holidays in Norway include **Syttende mai** (Constitution Day, May 17), which is celebrated across the country with parades, flags, music, dance and other festivities. **Sankthansaften** (St. John's Eve), Midsummer Night, is the longest night of the year and is also a fun event, traditionally celebrated with bonfires.

HOLIDAYS

January 1	**Første nyttårsdag**	New Year's Day
May 1	**Første mai**	May Day (Labor Day)
May 17	**Syttende mai**	Constitution Day
December 25	**Første juledag**	Christmas Day
December 26	**Annen juledag**	Boxing Day

MOVEABLE DATES

Maundy Thursday	**Skjærtorsdag**
Good Friday	**Langfredag**
Easter Sunday	**Første påskedag**
Easter Monday	**Annen påskedag**
Ascension Day	**Kristi himmelfartsdag**
Whit Sunday	**Første pinsedag**
Whit Monday	**Annen pinsedag**
St. John's Eve	**Sankthansaften**

Numerous festivals and cultural events are scheduled throughout the year in Norway, some with movable dates. Tourist offices, travel agencies, hotels and guidebooks offer extensive information about local and national celebrations. Many festivals are music oriented featuring folk, chamber and opera, with jazz music being especially popular.

ARRIVAL & DEPARTURE

NEED TO KNOW

I'm here on vacation [holiday]/business.
Jeg er her på ferie/i forretninger.
yay ar har paw feh´r • yuh/ih fohr • reht´ • nihng • uhr

I'm going to...
Jeg reiser til...
yay rays` • uhr tihl...

I'm staying at the... Hotel.
Jeg bor på Hotell...
yay boor paw hu • tehl´...

YOU MAY HEAR...

Billetten/Passet, takk.
bihl • leht´ • tuhn/ pahs´ • suh tahk

Your ticket/passport, please.

Hva er formålet med reisen?
vah ar fohr` • maw • luh meh ray` • suhn

What's the purpose of your trip?

Hvor skal du bo?
voor skahl dew boo

Where are you staying?

Hvor lenge blir du?
voor lehng` • uh bleer dew

How long are you staying?

Hvem reiser du sammen med?
vehm ray` • suhr dew sahm´ • muhn meh

Who are you with?

BORDER CONTROL

YOU MAY HEAR...

Har du noe å fortolle?
hahr dew noo` • uh aw fohr • tohl´ • luh

Do you have anything to declare?

Du må betale toll for dette.
dew maw buh • tah´ • luh tohl fohr deht` • tuh

You must pay duty on this.

Vær så snill å åpne denne bagen.
var saw snihl aw aw`p • nuh dehn` • nuh behg´ • guhn

Please open this bag.

Vekslingskontor
Exchange bureau

Bussterminalen
Bus terminal

T-bane
Metro

I'm just passing through.	**Jeg er bare på gjennomreise.**
	yay ar <u>bah</u>` • ruh paw
	<u>yehn</u>` • nohm • ray • suh
I would like to declare…	**Jeg vil gjerne fortolle…**
	yay vihl <u>ya</u>`r • nuh fohr • <u>tohl</u>´ • luh…
I have nothing to declare.	**Jeg har ingenting å fortolle.**
	yay hahr <u>ihng</u>` • uhn • tihng aw
	fohr • <u>tohl</u>´ • luh

MONEY

NEED TO KNOW

Where's…?	**Hvor er det…?**
	voor <u>ar</u> deh…
the ATM	**en minibank**
	ehn <u>mee</u>´ • nih • bangk
the bank	**en bank**
	ehn bahngk
the currency exchange office	**et vekslingskontor**
	eht <u>vehk</u>`s • lihngs • kun • toor
What time does the bank open/close?	**Når åpner/stenger banken?**
	nohr <u>aw</u>`p • nuhr/stehng` • uhr
	bahng´ • uhn
I'd like to change some dollars/pounds.	**Jeg vil gjerne veksle noen dollar/pund.**
	yay vihl <u>ya</u>`r • nuh <u>vehk</u>`s • luh
	<u>noo</u>` • uhn <u>dohl</u>´ • lahr/pewn
I'd like to cash a traveler's check [cheque].	**Jeg vil gjerne løse inn en reisesjekk.**
	yay vihl <u>ya</u>`r • nuh <u>lur</u>` • suh ihn ehn
	<u>ray</u>` • suh • shehk

AT THE BANK

> (i)
>
> The Norwegian currency is the **krone** (crown),
> abbreviated to **kr** or **NOK**, divided into 100 øre.
> Coins: 50 øre; **kr** 1, 5, 10 and 20
> Notes: **kr** 50, 100, 200, 500 and 1,000

Can I exchange foreign currency here?	**Kan jeg veksle utenlandsk valuta her?** *kahn yay <u>vehk`s</u> • luh <u>ew`</u> • tuhn • lahnsk vah • <u>lew´</u> • tah har*
What's the exchange rate?	**Hva er vekslingskursen?** *vah ar <u>vehk`s</u> • lihngs • kewr • suhn*
How much is the fee?	**Hvor mye tar dere i kommisjon?** *voor <u>mui`</u> • uh tahr deh` • ruh ih ku • mih • <u>shoo´</u>n*
I've lost my traveler's checks [cheques].	**Jeg har mistet reisesjekkene.** *yay hahr <u>mihs`</u> • tuht <u>ray`</u> • suh • shehk • kuh • nuh*
My card was lost.	**Jeg har mistet kortet.** *yay hahr <u>mihs`</u> • tuht <u>kohr´</u> • tuh*

My credit cards have been stolen.	**Kredittkortene mine ble stjålet.**
	kreh • diht´ • kohr • tuh • nuh mee` • nuh bleh styaw` • luht
My card doesn't work.	**Kortet virker ikke.**
	kohr´ • tuh vihr` • kuhr ihk` • kuh
The ATM ate my card.	**Minibanken spiste kortet mitt.**
	mee • nih • bangk • en spih • ste kurt • tuh miht

For Numbers, see page 22.

ⓘ

Cash can be obtained from **minibank** (ATMs), which can be readily found in urban areas . Most major credit cards and some debit cards are accepted. You will need a PIN that is compatible with European machines, usually a four-digit, numeric code. ATMs offer good rates, though there may be hidden fees.

Vekslingskontor (currency exchange offices), banks and post offices are options for exchanging currency. Exchange offices are found at airports, train stations, ship terminals and in many tourist centers. Banks are generally open Monday to Friday 8:15 a.m. to 3:30 p.m., though some close later one day a week and hours may vary in the provinces. Remember to bring your passport, in case you are asked for identification.

CONVERSATION

NEED TO KNOW

Hello/Hi!	**Hallo/Hei!** *hah • loo´/hay*
How are you?	**Hvordan står det til?** *voor´ • dahn stawr deh tihl*
Fine, thanks.	**Bare bra, takk.** *bah` • ruh brah tahk*
Excuse me.	**Unnskyld.** *ewn´ • shewl*
Do you speak	**Snakker du engelsk?** *snahk` • kuhr dew ehng´ • ehlsk*
What's your name?	**Hva heter du?** *vah heh` • tuhr dew*
My name is...	**Jeg heter...** *yay heh` • tuhr...*
Nice to meet you!	**Hyggelig å treffes!** *huig` • guh • lih aw trehf` • fuhs*
Where are you from?	**Hvor kommer du fra?** *voor kohm´ • muhr dew frah*
I'm from the U.S./ the U.K.	**Jeg er fra USA/Storbritannia.** *yay ar frah ew • ehs • ah´/ stoo´r • brih • tahn • yah*
What do you do?	**Hva jobber du med?** *vah yohb` • buhr dew meh*
I work for...	**Jeg jobber for...** *yay yohb` • buhr fohr...*
I'm a student.	**Jeg er student.** *yay ar stew • dehnt´*

I'm retired.	**Jeg er pensjonist.**
	yay ar pang • shu • nihst´
Do you like...?	**Liker du...?**
	lee´ • kuhr dew...
Goodbye.	**Adjø.**
	ahd • yur´
See you later.	**Vi ses.**
	vee seh` • uhs

LANGUAGE DIFFICULTIES

Do you speak English?	**Snakker du engelsk?**
	snahk` • kuhr dew ehng´ • uhlsk
Does anyone here speak English?	**Er det noen her som snakker engelsk?**
	ar deh noo` • uhn har sohm snahk` • kuhr ehng´ • uhlsk
I don't speak (much) Norwegian.	**Jeg snakker ikke (så bra) norsk.**
	yay snahk` • kuhr ihk` • kuh (saw brah) norsk
Could you speak more slowly?	**Kan du snakke litt langsommere?**
	kahn dew snahk` • kuh liht lahng` • sohm • muh • ruh
Could you repeat that?	**Kan du gjenta det?**
	kahn dew yehn´ • tah deh
Excuse me.	**Unnskyld.**
	ewn´ • shewl
What was that?	**Hva sa du?**
	vah sah dew
Can you write it down?	**Kan du skrive det?**
	kahn dew skree` • vuh deh
Can you translate this for me?	**Kan du oversette dette for meg?**
	kahn dew aw` • vuhr • seht • tuh deht` • tuh fohr may

What does this mean?	**Hva betyr dette?**
	vah buh • tui´r deht` • tuh
I (don't) understand.	**Jeg forstår (ikke).**
	yay for • staw´r (ihk` • kuh)
Do you understand?	**Forstår du?**
	for • staw´r dew

De (the formal form of 'you') is generally no longer used to address strangers, but is restricted to written works and addressing older people. As a general rule, **du** can be used in all situations without offending anyone.

YOU MAY HEAR...

Jeg snakker ikke engelsk.	I don't
yay snahk` • kuhr ihk` • kuh ehng´ • uhlsk	speak English.
Jeg snakker bare litt engelsk.	I only speak a
yay sahk • ehr bahr • eh liht ehn • gehlsk	little English.

MAKING FRIENDS

Hello/Hi!	**Hallo/Hei!**
	hah • loo´/hay
Good morning.	**God morgen.**
	gum • maw` • ruhn
Good afternoon.	**God dag.**
	gud • dah´g
Good evening.	**God aften/God kveld.**
	gu • ahf` • tuhn/guk • kvehl´
My name is...	**Jeg heter...**
	yay heh` • tuhr...

Can I introduce you to...?	**Kan jeg få presentere deg for...?** *kahn yay faw pre•sahng•teh´•ruh day fohr...*
Nice to meet you!	**Hyggelig å treffes!** *huig`•guh•lih oh trehf`•fuhs*
How are you?	**Hvordan står det til?** *voor´•dahn stawr deh tihl*
Fine, thanks.	**Bare bra, takk.** *bah`•ruh brah tahk*
And you?	**Og med deg?** *oh meh day*

TRAVEL TALK

I'm here...	**Jeg er her...** *yay ar har...*
on business	**i forretninger** *ih fohr•reht´•nihng•uhr*
on vacation [holiday]	**på ferie** *poh feh´r•yuh*
studying	**som student** *sohm stew•dehn´t*
I'm staying for...	**Jeg blir her...** *yay bleer har...*
I've been here...	**Jeg har vært her...** *yay hahr vehrt har...*
a day	**en dag** *ehn dahg*
a week	**en uke** *ehn ew`•kuh*
a month	**en måned** *ehn maw`•nuhd*
Where are you from?	**Hvor kommer du fra?** *voor kohm´-muhr dew frah*
I'm from...	**Jeg er fra...** *yay ar frah...*

For Numbers, see page 22.

PERSONAL

Who are you with?	**Hvem reiser du sammen med?**	
	vehm ray`-suhr dew sahm´-muhn meh	
I'm on my own.	**Jeg reiser alene.**	
	yay ray`-suhr ah-leh`-nuh	
I'm with…	**Jeg er her med…**	
	yay ar har meh…	
my husband/wife	**mannen min/kona mi**	
	mahn´-nuhn mihn/koo`-nah mih	
my boyfriend/ girlfriend	**kjæresten min**	
	kha`-reh-stuhn mihn	
a friend	**en venn**	
	ehn vehn	
a colleague	**en kollega**	
	ehn kohl-leh´-gah	
colleagues	**kolleger**	
	kul•ehg•ehr	
When's your birthday?	**Når har du bursdag?**	
	nohr hahr dew bew´rs-dahg	
How old are you?	**Hvor gammel er du?**	
	voor gahm`-muhl ar dew	
I'm…	**Jeg er…**	
	yay ar…	
Are you married?	**Er du gift?**	
	ar dew yihft	
I'm…	**Jeg er…**	
	yay ar…	
single	**ugift**	
	ew`•yihft	
in a relationship	**opptatt**	
	ohp´•taht	
engaged	**forlovet**	
	fawr•lawv•eht	

married	**gift**
	yihft
divorced	**skilt**
	shihlt
separated	**separert**
	seh • pah • reh´rt
I'm widowed.	**Jeg er enkemann** *m* **/enke** *f.*
	yay ar ehng` • kuh • mahn/ehng` • kuh
Do you have children/ grandchildren?	**Har du barn/barnebarn?**
	hahr dew bahrn/ bah`rn • uh • bahrn

WORK & SCHOOL

What do you do?	**Hva jobber du med?**
	vah yohb` • buhr dew meh
What are you studying?	**Hva studerer du?**
	vah stew • deh´ • ruhr dew
I'm studying…	**Jeg studerer…**
	yay stew • deh´ • ruhr…
I work full time/ part time.	**Jeg jobber fulltid/deltid.**
	yay yohb` • bur fewl´ • teed/dehl´ • teed
I am unemployed.	**Jeg er arbeidsledig.**
	yay ar ahr • bayds • leh • dihg
I work at home.	**Jeg jobber hjemmefra.**
	yay jawb • ehr yem • eh • frah
Who do you work for?	**Hvem jobber du for?**
	vehm yohb` • buhr dew fohr
I work for…	**Jeg jobber for…**
	yay yohb` • buhr fohr…
Here's my business card.	**Her er visittkortet mitt.**
	har ar vihs • iht´ • kor • tuh miht

WEATHER

What's the weather forecast?	**Hva sier værmeldingen?** *vah see`•uhr var`•mehl•lihng•uhn*
What beautiful weather!	**Så fint vær det er!** *soh feent var deh ar*
What terrible weather!	**For et forferdelig vær!** *fohr eht fohr•fehr´•duh•lih var*
It's cool/warm.	**Det er kjølig/varmt.** *deh ar khur`•lih/vahrmt*
It's snowy/icy.	**Det snør/er kaldt.** *deh snurr/ar kahlt*
It's rainy.	**Det regner.** *deh rayn`•uhr*
It's sunny.	**Sola skinner.** *soo´•lah shih´•nuhr*
Do I need a jacket/ an umbrella?	**Trenger jeg jakke/paraply?** *trehng´•uhr yay yahk`•kuh/ pah•rah•plui´*

For Seasons, see page 28.

EXPLORING

Lærdals-
tunnelen
24.5 km

GETTING AROUND

NEED TO KNOW

How do I get to town?	**Hvordan kommer jeg til byen?** _voor´_ • dahn _kohm´_ • muhr yay tihl _bui´_ • uhn
Where is…?	**Hvor er…?** _voor ar…_
the airport	**flyplassen** _flui´_ • plahs • suhn
the train station	**jernbanestasjonen** ya`rn • bah • nuh • stah • shoon • uhn
the bus station	**busstasjonen** bews´ • stah • shoon • uhn
the subway [underground] station	**T-banestasjonen** _teh´_ • bah • nuh • stah • shoon • uhn
How far is it?	**Hvor langt er det?** voor _lahngt_ _ar_ deh
Where can I buy tickets?	**Hvor kan jeg kjøpe billetter?** voor kahn yay _khur`_ • puh bihl • _leht´_ • tuhr

A one-way [single]/ round-trip [return] ticket.	**En enveisbillett/tur-returbillett.** *ehn ehn • vays • bihl • leht/ tewr • reh • tew´r • bil • leht*
How much?	**Hvor mye koster det?** *voor mui` • uh kohs` • tuhr deh*
Are there any discounts?	**Er det noen rabatter?** *ar deh noo` • uhn rah • baht´ • tuhr*
Which...?	**Hvilken...?** *vihl´ • kuhn...*
gate	**utgang** *ew`t • gahng*
line	**linje** *lihn` • yuh*
platform	**perrong** *pehr • rohng´*
Where can I get a taxi?	**Hvor kan jeg få tak i en drosje?** *voor kahn yay faw tahk ih ehn drohsh` • uh*
Can you take me to this address?	**Kan du kjøre meg til denne adressen?** *kahn dew khur` • ruh may tihl dehn` • nuh ahd • rehs` • suhn*
Where can I rent a car?	**Hvor kan jeg leie bil?** *voor kahn yay lay` • uh beel*
Can I have a map?	**Kan jeg få et kart?** *kahn yay faw eht kahrt*

TICKETS

When's...to Stavanger?	**Når går...til Stavanger?** *nohr gawr...tihl stah • vahng´ • uhr*
the (first) bus	**(første) buss** *(furrs` • tuh) bews*

the (next) flight	**(neste) fly**
	(nehs` • tuh) flui
the (last) train	**(siste) tog**
	(sihs` • tuh) tawg
Where can I buy tickets?	**Hvor kan jeg kjøpe billetter?**
	voor kahn yay khur` • puh bihl • leht´ • tuhr
One ticket/ please.	**En billett/To billetter, takk.**
	ehn bihl • leht´/too bihl • leht´ • tuhr tak
For today/tomorrow.	**For i dag/i morgen.**
	fohr ih • dahg/ih • mawr` • uhn
A one-way [single]/ round-trip [return] ticket.	**En enveisbillett/tur-returbillett.**
	ehn ehn´ • vays • bihl • leht/ tewr • reh • tew´r • bil • leht
A first class/ economy class ticket.	**En billett på første klasse/ turistklasse.**
	ehn bihl • eht´ poh furrs` • tuh klahs` • suh/tew • rihst´ • klahs • suh
How much?	**Hvor mye koster det?**
	voor mui` • uh kohs´ • tuhr deh
Is there a discount for...?	**Er det noen rabatt for...?**
	ar deh noo` • uhn rah • baht´ fohr...
children	**barn**
	bahrn

YOU MAY HEAR...

Hvilket selskap flyr du med?
vihl´ • kuht sehl` • skahp fluir dew meh
Innenlands eller utenlands?
ihn` • nuhn • lahns
ehl´ • luhr ew` • tuhn • lahns
Hvilken terminal?
vihl´ • kuhn tehr • mih • nahl´

What airline are you flying?
Domestic or international?

What terminal?

students	**studenter**	
	stew • dehn´ • tuhr	
senior citizens	**pensjonister**	
	pahng • shoo • nihs´ • tuhr	
The express bus/ express train, please.	**Ekspressbuss/ekspresstog, er du snill**	
	eks • pruhs • bews/eks • pruhs • tawg, ar dew snihl	
The local bus/train, please.	**Lokalbuss/-tog, er du snill.**	
	loh • kahl • bews/tawg, ar dew snihl	
I have an e-ticket.	**Jeg har en e-billett.**	
	yay hahr ehn eh´ • bihl • leht	
Can I buy a ticket on the bus/train?	**Kan man kjøpe billett på bussen/toget?**	
	kahn mahn khur` • puh bihl • leht´ poh bews´ • suhn/taw´ • guh	
Do I have to stamp the ticket before boarding?	**Må jeg stemple billetten før jeg går ombord?**	
	maw yay stam • pleh bill • eht • ehn fur yay gawr awm • bohr	
How long is this ticket valid?	**Hvor lenge er denne billetten gyldig?**	
	voor lehn • geh ar dehn • neh beel • eht • ehn yil • deeg	

Can I return on the same ticket?	**Er det tur/retur?**
	ar deh tewr/reh • tewr
I'd like to...my reservation.	**Jeg vil gjerne...reservasjonen.**
	yay vihl ya`r • nuh...
	reh • sehr • vah • shoo´n • uhn
cancel	**annullere**
	ahn • newl • leh´ • ruh
change	**endre**
	ehn` • druh
confirm	**bekrefte**
	buh • krehf´ • tuh

For Days, see page 26.

AIRPORT TRANSFER

How much is a taxi to the airport?	**Hva koster drosje til flyplassen?**
	vah kohs` • tuhr drohsh` • uh tihl
	flui´ • plahs • suhn
To...Airport, please.	**Til...lufthavn.**
	tihl...lewft´ • hahvn
My airline is...	**Jeg flyr med...**
	yay fluir meh...

My flight leaves at...	**Flyet mitt går...**
	flui´ • uh miht gawr...
I'm in a hurry.	**Jeg har dårlig tid.**
	yay hahr dawr` • lih teed
Can you take an alternate route?	**Kan du kjøre en annen vei?**
	kahn dew _khur`_ • ruh ehn _ahn´_ • nuhn vay
Can you drive faster/slower?	**Kan du kjøre fortere/saktere?**
	kahn dew _khur`_ • ruh _foor`_ • tuh • ruh/ _sahk`_ • tuh • ruhw

For Time, see page 25.

YOU MAY SEE...

ANKOMST	arrivals
AVGANG	departures
BAGASJEBÅND	baggage claim
SIKKERHETSVAKT	security
INNENLAND	domestic flights
UTLAND	international flights
INNSJEKKING	check-in
INNSJEKKING MED E-BILLETT	e-ticket check-in
GATE FOR AVGANG	departure gates

CHECKING IN

Where's check-in?	**Hvor er innsjekkingsskranken?**
	voor ar _ihn´_ • shehk • kihngs • skrahng • kuhn
My name is...	**Jeg heter...**
	yay _heh`_ • tuhr...
I'm going to...	**Jeg skal til...**
	yay skahl tihl...

I have...	**Jeg har...**
	yay hahr
one suitcase	**en koffert**
	ehn kohf•uhrt
two suitcases	**to kofferter**
	toh kohf•uhrt•uhr
one piece of hand luggage	**en håndbagasje**
	ehn hawn•bahg•ahsh•uh
How much luggage is allowed?	**Hvor mye bagasje har man lov å ha med?**
	voor <u>mui</u>`•uh bah•<u>gah´</u>•shuh hahr mahn lawv oh hah meh
Is that pounds or kilos?	**Er det i pund eller kilo?**
	ar deht•uh ee pewn ehl•uhr shee•loh
Which terminal?	**Hvilken terminal?**
	vee'k•uhn tar•mihn•ahl
Which gate?	**Hvilken gate?**
	vee'k•uhn gayt
Can I have a window/an aisle seat?	**Kan jeg få plass ved vinduet/midtgangen?**
	kahn yay faw plahs veh <u>vihn</u>`•dew•uh/<u>miht</u>`•gahng•uhn

YOU MAY HEAR...

Neste!
nehs` • _tuh_

Next!

Billetten/Passet, takk.
bil • _leht´_ • _tuhn/pahs´_ • _suh tahk_

Your ticket/
passport, please.

Hvor mange kolli har du?
voor _mang`_ • _uh_ _kohl´_ • _lih_ _hahr dew_

How many
pieces of luggage
do you have?

Du har for mye bagasje.
dew hahr fohr _mui´_ • _uh bah_ • _gah´_ • _shuh_

You have excess
luggage.

Den er for tung/stor til håndbagasje.
dehn ar fohr tung/stoor tihl
hohn` • _bah_ • _gah´_ • _shuh_

That's too
heavy/large for
a carry-on [to
carry on board].

**Har du pakket disse veskene/
koffertene selv?**
hahr dew pahk`_ • _kuht dihs` • _suh_
vehs` • _kuh_ • _nuh/kuf´_ • _fuhr_ • _tuh_ • _nuh_
sehl

Did you pack
these bags/
suitcases
yourself?

Tar du med noe for andre?
tahr _dew meh_ _noo`_ • _uh fohr_ _ahn`_ • _druh_

Did anyone give
you anything to
carry?

Tøm lommene.
turm _lum`_ • _muh_ • _nuh_

Empty your
pockets.

Ta av deg skoene.
tah ah day _skoo´_ • _uh_ • _nuh_

Take off your
shoes.

Avgang...er nå klar for ombordstigning.
ahv` • _gahng...ar naw klahr fohr_
ohm • _boor´_ • _steeg_ • _nihng_

Now boarding
flight...

When do we leave/ arrive?	**Når drar vi/kommer vi fram?**
	nohr dr<u>ah</u>r v<u>ee</u>/k<u>oh</u>m´ • muhr v<u>ee</u> frahm
Is the flight delayed?	**Er flyet forsinket?**
	ar <u>flui</u>´ • uh fohr • s<u>ihng</u>´ • kuht
How late will it be?	**Hvor sent vil det bli?**
	voor s<u>eh</u>nt vihl deh bl<u>ee</u>

LUGGAGE

Where is/are...?	**Hvor er...?**
	voor ar...
the luggage carts [trolleys]	**bagasjetrallene**
	bah • <u>gah</u>´ • shuh • trahl • luh • nuh
the luggage lockers	**oppbevaringsboksene**
	<u>ohp</u>´ • buh • vah • rihngs • bohk • suh • nuh
the baggage claim	**bagasjeutleveringen**
	bah • <u>gah</u>´ • shuh • ewt • leh • veh • ri hng • uhn
My luggage has been lost/stolen.	**Bagasjen min er tapt/stjålet.**
	bah • ahsh • uhn mihn ar tahpt/stjawl • uht
My suitcase was damaged.	**Kofferten min ble skadet.**
	<u>kuf</u>´ • fuhr • tuhn mihn bl<u>eh</u> <u>skah</u>` • duht

FINDING YOUR WAY

Where is...?	**Hvor er...?**
	voor ar...
the currency exchange office	**vekslingskontoret**
	vehks` • lihngs • kun • too • ruh
the exit	**utgangen**
	ewt` • gahng • uhn
the taxi stand [rank]	**drosjeholdeplassen**
	drohsh` • uh • hol • luh • plahs • suhn
the car hire	**bilutleie**
	beel • ewt • lay • eh
Is there... into town?	**Går det... inn til byen?**
	gawr deh... ihn tihl by • ehn
a bus	**en buss**
	ehn bews
a train	**et tog**
	eht tawg
an underground station	**en T-bane**
	ehn teh • bahn • eh

For Asking Directions, see page 64.

YOU MAY HEAR...

Ta plass.	All aboard.
tah plahs	
Billetter, takk.	Tickets, please.
bihl • leht´ • tuhr tahk	
Du må bytte i...	You have to
dew maw buit` • tuh ih...	change at...
Neste holdeplass...	Next stop...
nehs` • tuh hohl` • luh • plahs...	

TRAIN

How do I get to the train station?	**Hvordan kommer jeg til jernbanestasjonen?**
	voor´•dahn kohm´•muhr yay tihl ya`rn•bah•nuh•stah•shoo•nuhn
Is it far from here?	**Er det langt herfra?**
	ar deh lahngt ha´r•frah
Where is/are...?	**Hvor er...?**
	voor ar...
the ticket office	**billettluken**
	bihl•leht´•lew•kuhn
the information desk	**informasjonsskranken**
	ihn•fohr•mah•shoo´ns•skrahng•kuhn
the platforms	**perrongene**
	par•awng•ehn•uh
the luggage lockers	**bagasjeskapene**
	bahg•ahsh•uh•skahp•ehn•uh
Can I have a train schedule [timetable]?	**Kan jeg få en togtabell?**
	kahn yay faw ehn tawg`•tah•behl
How long is the trip?	**Hvor lang er turen?**
	voor lang ar tew´•ruhn
Is it a direct train?	**Går toget direkte?**
	gawr tawg•eht deeh•rehk•teh
Do I have to change trains?	**Må jeg bytte tog?**
	maw yay buit`•tuh taw
Is the train on time?	**Er toget i rute?**
	ar tawg•eht ee rewt•eh

For Tickets, see page 45.

Norway runs a train network more than 4,000 km (c. 2,500 miles) long, though the system is much more comprehensive in the south than the north. Oslo is the main hub for most long-distance, express and local trains. Long-distance lines that span the country are an excellent way to view the incredible Norwegian scenery.

A number of discounts are available: children under 4 travel free of charge, and children under 16 and senior citizens travel at half price. Local buses, trams, subways and ferries run on an integrated network, so you may transfer at no additional cost. Keep in mind that buying a **flexikort** (multi-trip ticket) is cheaper than buying single tickets. For moving around the capital, you may also want to consider a 1-, 2- or 3-day (children's or family) **Oslo Pass**, which offers unlimited public transportation within greater Oslo and free entry to a number of museums and tourist attractions. For long-distance travel, passes such as Eurorail (non-European residents), InterRail (European residents) or ScanRail (for travel within Scandinavia) can offer better value fares.

DEPARTURES

Which track [platform] does the train to Skien leave from?	**Fra hvilket spor går toget til Skien?** *frah vihl´ • kuht spoor gawr taw´ • guh til sheh • uhn*
Is this the track [platform] to…?	**Er dette sporet til…?** *ar deht` • tuh spoo´ • ruh tihl…*
Where is track [platform]…?	**Hvor er spor…?** *voor ar spoor…*
Where do I change for…?	**Hvor må jeg bytte for å komme til…?** *voor maw yay buit` • tuh fohr aw kohm` • muh tihl…*

ON BOARD

Is this seat taken?	**Er denne plassen opptatt?** *<u>ar</u> dehn` • nuh <u>plahs</u>´ • suhn <u>ohp</u>´ • taht*
Can I sit here?	**Kan jeg sitte her?** *kahn yay siht • uh har*
Can I open the window?	**Kan jeg åpne vinduet?** *kahn yay awpn • eh vihn • dew • eh*
I think that's my seat.	**Jeg tror at det er min plass.** *yay troor aht deh ar meen plahs*
Here's my reservation.	**Her er reservasjonen min.** *har ar rehs • ehr • vahsh • un • uhn mihn*

BUS

YOU MAY SEE...

BUSSHOLDEPLASS/ **TRIKKEHOLDEPLASS**	bus stop/train stop
STOPP	request stop
INNGANG/UTGANG	enter/exit
STEMPLE BILLETTEN	stamp your ticket

Where's the bus station?	**Hvor er busstasjonen?** *voor ar <u>bews´</u>•sta•shoo•nuhn*
How far is it?	**Hvor langt er det?** *voor <u>lahngt</u> **ar** deh*
How do I get to…?	**Hvordan kommer jeg til…?** *<u>voor´</u>•dahn <u>kohm´</u>•muhr yay tihl…*
Does the bus/train stop at (place/ area)…?	**Stopper bussen/trikken (ved/på)…?** *<u>stohp´</u>•puhr <u>bews´</u>•suhn/<u>trihk´</u>•kuhn (veh/poh)…*
Can you tell me when to get off?	**Kan du si meg når jeg skal av?** *kahn dew see may nohr yay skahl **ah***
Do I have to change buses?	**Må jeg bytte buss?** *maw yay <u>buit`</u>•tuh bews*
Can you stop here?	**Kan du stoppe her?** *kahn dew <u>stohp`</u>•puh har*

For Tickets, see page 45.

T-BANE

(i)

The Oslo **Tunnelbane** or **T-bane** (subway) runs from approximately 5:30 a.m. to just after midnight. Buying a **flexikort** (multi-trip ticket) is a good idea if you plan on making numerous trips. It can be used to make transfers within one hour at no extra charge. An **Oslo Pass** is another discount travel pass, good for all forms of public transportation.

Where's the nearest subway [underground] station?	**Hvor er nærmeste T-banestasjon?** *voor ar <u>nar`</u>•mehs•tuh <u>teh´</u>•bah•nuh•stah•shoon*

Can I have a map of the subway [underground]?	**Kan jeg få et kart over T-banen?**
	kahn yay faw eht kart aw´•vuhr teh´•bah•nuh
Which line for…?	**Hvilken linje går til…?**
	vihl´•kuhn lihn`•yuh gawr tihl…
Which direction?	**Hvilken retning?**
	vee'k•ehn reht•nihng
Where do I change for…?	**Hvor må jeg bytte for å komme til…?**
	voor maw yay buit`•tuh fohr aw kohm`•muh tihl…
Is this the right train for…?	**Er dette toget til… ?**
	ar deht`•tuh taw´•guh tihl…
How many stops to…	**Hvor mange stoppesteder er det før…?**
	voor mahn•geh stohp•puh•steh•duhr ar deh fur
Where are we?	**Hvor er vi?**
	voor ar vee

For Finding your Way, see page 53.

BOAT & FERRY

| When does the boat/ferry for…leave? | **Når går båten/fergen til…?** |
| | *nohr gawr baw´•tuhn/fehr`•guhn tihl…* |

Can I take my car?	**Kan jeg ta med bilen?**
	kahn yay tah`• meh <u>bee</u>´• luhn
What time is the next sailing?	**Når er neste avgang?**
	nawr ar nehs • tuh ahv • gahng
Can I book a seat/cabin?	**Kan jeg bestille en plass/lugar?**
	kahn yay behs • tihl • uh ehn plahs/lewg • ahr
How long is the crossing?	**Hvor lang er overfarten?**
	voor lahng ar awv • ehr • fahrt • ehn

For Weather, see page 41.

Ferry and boat travel is efficient in Norway. Most ferries and high-speed ships have frequent departure schedules, so you rarely have to wait in lines, and the cost for passenger and car transport is generally low. Besides regular ferry service, several companies offer cruises along the fjords. These are very popular during the summer months and tickets are more expensive during this period, so reservations should be made well in advance.

TAXI

Where can I get a taxi?	**Hvor kan jeg få tak i en drosje?**
	voor kahn yay faw tahk ih ehn <u>droh</u>`• shuh
I'd like a taxi now/for tomorrow at…	**Jeg trenger en drosje nå/i morgen klokken…**
	yay <u>trehng</u>´• uhr ehn <u>droh</u>`• shuh n<u>aw</u>/ih <u>mawr</u>`• uhn <u>klohk</u>`• kuhn…
Can you pick me up…?	**Kan du hente meg…?**
	kahn dew <u>hehn</u>`• tuh may…
at the airport	**på flyplassen**
	poh fl<u>ui</u>´• plahs • suhn

Taxis can be hailed in the street, found at taxi stands or ordered by phone. All cabs are metered and service charges are included in the fare. You can tip the driver by rounding up the fare. Keep in mind that rates differ from place to place and travel by taxi is generally expensive, so ask for an approximate fare beforehand. Most taxis accept credit cards but be sure to double check first.

at the ferry landing	**ved fergeleiet**	
	veh fer`•guh•lay•uh	
at eight o'clock	**klokken åtte**	
	klohk`•kuhn oht`•tuh	
Take me to…	**Kjør meg til…**	
	khurr may tihl…	
this address	**denne adressen**	
	dehn`•nuh ahd•rehs´•suhn	
the airport	**flyplassen**	
	flui´•plahs•suhn	
the train station	**jernbanestasjonen**	
	ya`rn•bah•nuh•stah•shoon•uhn	

I'm in a hurry.	**Jeg har dårlig tid.**
	yay hahr dawr`•lih teed
Can you drive faster/ slower?	**Kan du kjøre fortere/saktere?**
	kahn dew khur`•ruh
	fohr`•tuh•ruh/sahk`•tuh•ruh
Stop/Wait here.	**Stopp/Vent her.**
	stohp/vehnt har
How much?	**Hvor mye koster det?**
	voor mui•uh kohs`•tuhr deh
You said…crowns.	**Du sa…kroner.**
	dew sah…kroo`•nuhr
Can I have a receipt?	**Kan jeg få en kvittering?**
	kahn yay faw ehn kviht•teh´•rihng
Keep the change.	**Behold vekslepengene.**
	buh•hohl´ vehk`s•luh•pehng•uh•nuh

YOU MAY HEAR…

Hvor skal du?
voor skahl dew

Where to?

Hva var adressen?
vah vahr ahd•rehs´•suhn

What's the address?

BICYCLE & MOTORBIKE

I'd like to rent [hire]…	**Jeg vil gjerne leie…**
	yay vihl ya`r•nuh lay`•uh…
a bicycle	**en sykkel**
	ehn suik´•kuhl
a moped	**en moped**
	ehn mu•peh´d
a motorcycle	**en motorsykkel**
	ehn moo´•toor•suik•kuhl

How much per day/week?	**Hvor mye koster det per dag/uke?**
	voor mui` • uh kohs` • tuhr deh pehr dahg/ew` • kuh
Can I have a helmet/lock?	**Kan jeg få med hjelm/lås?**
	kahn yay faw` • meh yehlm/laws

(i)

If you enjoy cycling there are many well-planned routes throughout the country, through lush valleys and breath-taking fjords. Attractions are usually signposted. You can bring your own bike or rent one easily. Given the terrain, a **terrengsykkel** (mountain bike) is usually the most practical option.

CAR HIRE

Where can I rent a car?	**Hvor kan jeg leie en bil?**
	voor kahn yay lay` • uh ehn beel
I'd like to rent [hire]...	**Jeg vil gjerne leie...**
	yay vihl ya`r • nuh lay` • uh...
a 2-/4-door car	**en to-dørs/firedørs bil**
	ehn too´ • durrs/fee´ • ruh • durrs beel
an automatic	**en bil med automatgir**
	meh ev • tu • mah´t • geer
a car with air conditioning	**en bil med klimaanlegg**
	ehn beel meh klee´ • mah • ahn • lehg
a car seat	**et barnesete**
	eht bahr` • nuh • seh • tuh
a cheap/small car	**en billig/liten bil**
	ehn bihl • ih/liht • ehn beel
How much...?	**Hvor mye koster det...?**
	voor mui` • uh kohs` • tuhr deh...
per day	**per dag**
	pehr dahg
per week	**per uke**
	pehr ew` • kuh

per kilometer	**per kilometer**	
	pehr <u>khee</u>´• lu • meh • tuhr	
for unlimited mileage	**for ubegrenset kjørelengde**	
	fohr <u>ew</u>`• buh • grehn • suht	
	<u>khur</u>`• ruh • lehng • duh	
with insurance	**inkludert forsikring**	
	ihn • klew • <u>dehrt</u>´ fohr • <u>sihk</u>´• rihng	
Are there any discounts?	**Er det noen rabatter?**	
	ar deh noo`• uhn rah • <u>baht</u>´• tuhr	

YOU MAY HEAR...

Har du et internasjonalt førerkort?	Do you have an
<u>hahr</u> dew eht <u>ihn</u>´• tuhr • nah • shu • <u>nahlt</u>	international
<u>fur</u>`• ruhr • kohrt	driver's license?
Kan jeg få se passet?	Can I see your
kahn yay faw seh <u>pahs</u>´• suh	passport?
Vil du ha forsikring?	Do you want
vihl dew hah fohr • <u>sihk</u>´• rihng	insurance?
Det er et depositum på...	There is a
deh ar eht deh • <u>poo</u>´• sih • tewm poh...	deposit of...
Undertegn her.	Please sign here.
<u>ewn</u>`• nuhr • tayn har	

FUEL STATION

YOU MAY SEE...

NORMAL 95 OKTAN	regular
SUPER 98 OKTAN	premium [super]
DIESEL	diesel

Where's the nearest gas [petrol] station?	**Hvor er nærmeste bensinstasjon?**
	voor ar ner` • mehs • tuh behn • seen` • stah • shoon
Fill it up, please.	**Full tank, takk.**
	fewl tahngk tahk
...liters, please.	**...liter bensin, takk.**
	...lee´ • tuhr behn • seen´ tahk
Can I pay in cash/ by credit card?	**Kan jeg betale kontant/med kredittkort?**
	kahn yay buh • tah´ • luh kun • tahn´t / meh kreh • diht´ • kohrt

For Numbers, see page 22.

ASKING DIRECTIONS

Are we on the right road for...?	**Er dette veien til...?**
	ar deht` • tuh vay` • uhn tihl...
How far is it to...?	**Hvor langt er det til...?**
	voor lahngt ar deh tihl...
Where's...?	**Hvor er...?**
	voor ar...
...Street	**...gate**
	...gah` • tuh
this address	**denne adressen**
	dehn` • nuh ahd • rehs´ • suhn
the highway [motorway]	**motorveien**
	moo´ • toor • vay • uhn
Can you show me where I am on the map?	**Kan du vise meg på kartet hvor jeg er?**
	kahn dew vee` • suh may paw kahr´ • tuh voor yay ar
I'm lost.	**Jeg har gått meg vill.**
	yay hahr goht may vihl

YOU MAY HEAR...

rett frem	straight ahead
reht frehm	
på venstre side	on the left
poh <u>vehn</u>´ • struh <u>see</u>` • duh	
på høyre side	on the right
poh <u>hury</u>´ • ruh <u>see</u>` • duh	
på/rundt hjørnet	on/around the
poh/rewnt <u>yurr</u>` • nuh	corner
midt imot...	opposite...
miht ih • m<u>oo</u>t´...	
bak...	behind...
b<u>a</u>hk...	
ved siden av...	next to...
veh <u>see</u>` • duhn ah...	
etter...	after...
<u>eht</u>` • tuhr...	
nord/sør	north/south
n<u>oo</u>r/s<u>urr</u>	
øst/vest	east/west
urst/vehst	
ved lyskrysset	at the traffic light
veh <u>lui</u>`s • kruis • suh	
ved veikrysset	at the
veh <u>vay</u>` • kruis • suh	intersection

PARKING

> (i)
>
> Parking in Norway is restricted, particularly on weekdays. The most common system is the **P-automat** (automated parking meter) when you park your car, then pay for an amount of time at the meter; the meter then prints a ticket to be displayed on your dashboard. Another option is a **P-hus** (parking garage) when you receive a ticket upon entering the garage. Before getting into your car to leave the garage, you must pay for your ticket at an automated machine or a manned booth.

Can I park here?	**Kan jeg parkere her?**
	kahn yay pahr • keh´ • ruh har
Is there a parking lot [car park] nearby?	**Fins det en parkeringsplass i nærheten?**
	fins deh ehn pahr • keh´ • rihngs • plahs ih nar´ • heh • tuhn
How much…?	**Hvor mye koster det…?**
	voor mui` • uh kohs` • tuhr deh…
per hour	**per time**
	pehr tee` • muh
per day	**per dag**
	pehr dahg
for overnight	**over natten**
	aw´ • vuhr naht´ • tuhn

YOU MAY HEAR...

STOP	**STOPP**	stop
▽	**VIKEPLIKT**	yield
🚫	**PARKERING FORBUDT**	no parking
⬅	**ÉNVEISKJØRING**	one way
⊖	**INNKJØRING FORBUDT**	no entry
🚗	**FORBIKJØRING FORBUDT**	no passing
↩	**U-SVING FORBUDT**	no U-turn
🚸	**GANGFELT**	pedestrian crossing

BREAKDOWN & REPAIR

My car broke down/ won't start.	**Bilen har fått motorstopp/starter ikke.** _bee´ • luhn hahr foht moo´ • toor • stohp/ stahr` • tuhr ihk` • kuh_
Can you fix it (today)?	**Kan du reparere den i dag?** _kahn dew reh • pah • reh´ • ruh dehn ee dahg_

When will it be ready?	**Når er den klar?**
	nohr ar dehn klahr
How much?	**Hvor mye koster det?**
	*voor **mui**`•uh **kohs**`•tuhr deh*
I have a puncture/ flat tyre.	**Jeg har punktert/et flatt dekk.**
	yay hahr punk•tehrt/ eht flaht dehk

For Time, see page 25.

ACCIDENTS

There's been an accident.	**Det har skjedd en ulykke.**
	*deh hahr shehd ehn **ew**`•lui•kuh*
Call a doctor/an ambulance!	**Ring etter lege/sykebil!**
	*rihng **eht**`•tuhr **leh**`•guh/ **sui**`•kuh•b**eel***

For Police, see page 139.

PLACES TO STAY

NEED TO KNOW

Can you recommend a hotel?	**Kan du anbefale et hotell?** _kahn dew ahn´•buh•fah•luh eht hu•tehl´_
I have a reservation.	**Jeg har bestilt rom.** _yay hahr buh•stihlt´ rum_
My name is…	**Jeg heter…** _yay heh`•tuhr…_
Do you have a room…?	**Har dere et rom…?** _hahr deh`•ruh eht rum…_
for one/two	**for én/to** _fohr ehn/too_
with a bathroom	**med bad** _meh bahd_
with air conditioning	**med klimaanlegg** _meh klee´•mah•ahn•lehg_
For tonight.	**For i natt.** _fohr ih naht_
For two nights.	**For to netter.** _fohr too neht´•tuhr_
For one week.	**For en uke.** _fohr ehn ew`•kuh_
How much?	**Hvor mye koster det?** _voor mui`•uh kohs`•tuhr deh_
Do you have anything cheaper?	**Har dere noe rimeligere?** _hahr deh`•ruh noo`•uh ree`•muh•lih•uh•ruh_
When's check-out?	**Når må jeg sjekke ut?** _nohr maw yay shehk`•kuh ewt_

Can I leave this in the safe?	**Kan jeg legge denne/dette igjen i safen?**
	kahn yay <u>lehg</u>` • guh <u>dehn</u>` • nuh/<u>deht</u>` • tuh ih • <u>yehn</u>´ ih sayf´ • uhn
Can I leave my bags?	**Kan jeg sette igjen bagasjen?**
	kahn yay <u>seht</u>` • tuh ih • <u>yehn</u>´ bah • <u>gah</u>´ • shuhn
Can I have the bill/ a receipt?	**Kan jeg få regningen/en kvittering?**
	kahn yay faw <u>ray</u>` • ning • uhn/ehn kviht • <u>teh</u>´ • rihng
I'll pay in cash/by credit card.	**Jeg betaler kontant/med kredittkort.**
	yay buh • <u>tah</u>´ • luhr kun • <u>tahnt</u>´/meh <u>kreh</u> • diht´ • <u>kohrt</u>

SOMEWHERE TO STAY

Can you recommend...?	**Kan du anbefale...?**
	kahn dew <u>ahn</u>´ • buh • fah • luh
a bed and breakfast	**et rom inklusive frokost**
	eht rum ihnk • lews • ihv • eh fru • kawst
a campsite	**en campingplass**
	ehn kamp • ihng • plahs

ℹ️

In Norway, there are a variety of accommodation alternatives in addition to more conventional options such as hotels, bed and breakfasts or **husrom** (rooms in private houses) and **vandrerhjem** (hostels). For a unique holiday experience you could consider a **bondegårdsferie** (farm stay), which lets you taste Norwegian farm life firsthand. Similarly, along the coast, you could arrange to stay in **rorbuer** (fisherman's cabins). **Hytter** (chalets or cabins) are available throughout the country as well.

a hostel	**et hospits**
	eht hus • pihts
a hotel	**et hotel**
	eht hu • tehl´
What is it near?	**Hva er det i nærheten?**
	vah ar deh ih nar´ • heh • tuhn
How do I get there?	**Hvordan kommer jeg dit?**
	voor´ • dahn kohm´ • muhr yay deet

ℹ️

If you didn't reserve a room before your arrival, the local tourist office can provide information and help you to arrange a reservation. The official website of the Norwegian Tourist Board, Visit Norway (www.visitnorway.com), can provide information about locations in particular cities.

AT THE HOTEL

I have a reservation.	**Jeg har bestilt rom.**
	yay hahr buh • stihlt´ rum
My name is…	**Jeg heter…**
	yay heh` • tuhr…

Do you have a room…?	**Har dere et rom…?**
	hahr deh` • ruh eht rum…
with a bathroom/ shower	**med bad/dusj**
	meh bahd/dewsh
with a private toilet	**med toalett**
	meh tu • ah • leht
with air conditioning	**med klimaanlegg**
	meh klee´ • mah • ahn • lehg
that's smoking/ non-smoking	**for røykere/ikke-røykere**
	fohr ruryk` • uh • ruh/ ihk` • kuh • ruryk • uhr • uh
For…	**For…**
	fawr
tonight	**i natt**
	ee naht
two nights	**to netter**
	tu neht • ehr
a week	**en uke**
	ehn ewk • eh
Can I access the internet?	**Kan jeg bruke internett?**
	kahn yay brew` • kuh ihn´ • tuhr • neht
Does the hotel have…?	**Har hotellet…?**
	hahr hu • tehl´ • uh…
a computer	**en datamaskin**
	ehn dah´ • tah • mah • sheen
(wireless) internet service	**(trådløst) Internett**
	trawd • lurst ihnt • ar • neht
an elevator [lift]	**heis**
	hays
room service	**romservice**
	rum` • sur • vihs
a gym	**trimrom**
	trihm´ • rum
a pool	**et basseng**
	eht bahs • ehng

I need…	**Jeg trenger…**
	yay <u>trehng</u>´•uhr…
an extra bed	**en ekstra seng**
	ehn <u>ehks</u>´•trah sehng
a cot [camp bed]	**en feltseng**
	ehn <u>fehlt</u>´•sehng
a crib [child's cot]	**en barneseng**
	ehn <u>bahr</u>`•nuh•sehng

Norwegian electricity is generally 220 volts and round two-pin plugs are typically used. British and American appliances may need an adapter.

YOU MAY SEE…

SKYV/TREKK	push/pull
TOALETT	restroom [toilet]
DUSJ	shower
HEIS	elevator [lift]
TRAPP	stairs
VAREAUTOMATER	vending machines
IS	ice
VASKERI	laundry
IKKE FORSTYRR	do not disturb
BRANNDØR	fire door
NØDUTGANG	emergency/fire exit
VEKKING	wake-up call

PRICE

How much per night/week?	**Hvor mye koster det per natt/uke?** *voor mui` • uh kohs` • tuhr deh pehr naht/ ew` • kuh*
Does the price include breakfast/ sales tax [VAT]?	**Er frokost/moms inkludert i prisen?** *ar froo´ • kust/mums ihn • klu • dehrt´ ih pree´ • suhn*
Are there any discounts?	**Har dere noen rabatter?** *hahr dehr • eh nu • ehn rah • baht • ehr*

PREFERENCES

Can I see the room?	**Kan jeg få se rommet?** *kahn yay faw seh paw rum • eht*
I'd like a...room.	**Jeg vil gjerne ha et...rom.** *yay vihl yar • neh hah eht...rum*
better	**bedre** *beh • dreh*
bigger	**større** *stur • reh*
cheaper	**billigere** *bihl • ihg • ehr • eh*
quieter	**roligere** *ru • lihg • ehr • eh*

I'll take it.	**Jeg tar det.**
	yay tahr deh
No, I won't take it.	**Nei, jeg vil ikke ha det.**
	nai, yay vihl ihk • eh hah deh

QUESTIONS

YOU MAY HEAR...

Passet/kredittkortet ditt, takk.	Your passport/
<u>pah</u>´ • suh/ kreh • <u>diht</u>´ • kohr • tuh	credit card,
diht tahk	please.
Kan du fylle ut dette skjemaet?	Can you fill out
kahn dew <u>fui</u>` • luh ewt <u>deht</u>` • tuh	this form?
sheh<u>eh</u>´ • mah • uh	
Undertegn her.	Sign here.
<u>ewn</u>` • nuhr • tayn har	

Where's...?	**Hvor er...?**
	voor ar...
the bar	**baren**
	<u>bah</u>´ • ruhn

the bathroom	**toalettet**
	tu • ah • leht´ • uh
the elevator [lift]	**heisen**
	hay´ • suhn
Can I have…?	**Kan jeg få…?**
	kahn yay faw…
a blanket	**et ullteppe**
	eht ewl` • tehp • puh
an iron	**et strykejern**
	eht strui` • kuh • yarn
a pillow	**en pute**
	ehn pew` • tuh
the room key/ key card	**romnøkkelen/nøkkelkortet?**
	rum • nurk • ehl • ehn/nurk • ehl • kurt • eht
a soap	**en såpe**
	ehn saw` • puh
toilet paper	**toalettpapir**
	tu • ah • leht´ • pah • peer
a towel	**et håndkle**
	eht hohng` • kleh
Do you have an adapter for this?	**Har du en adapter til denne/dette?**
	hahr dew ehn ahd • ahp´ • tuhr tihl dehn` • nuh/deht´ • tuh
How do I turn on the lights?	**Hvordan slår jeg på lyset?**
	voor´ • dahn slawr yay poh lui´s • uh
Can you wake me at…?	**Kan du vekke meg klokken…?**
	kahn dew vehk` • kuh may klohk` • kuhn…
Can I leave this in the safe?	**Kan jeg få legge denne i safen?**
	kahn yay faw lehg • eh dehn • eh ee sayf • ehn
Could I have my things from the safe?	**Kan jeg få sakene mine fra safen?**
	kahn yay faw sah` • kuh • nuh mee` • nuh frah say´ • fuhn

Is/are there any mail/messages for me?	**Har det kommet noe post/ noen beskjed til meg?** *hahr deh kohm` • muht noo` • uh pohst/noo` • uhn buh • sheh´ tihl may*
Do you have a laundry service?	**Har dere vaskeritjenester?** *hahr dehr • uh vahsk • ehr • ee • tjehn • ehst • uhr*

PROBLEMS

There's a problem.	**Jeg har et problem.** *yay hahr eht pru • bleh´m*
I've lost my key/ key card.	**Jeg har mistet nøkkelen/nøkkelkortet.** *yay hahr mihs` • tuht nurk` • kehl • uhn/ nurk` • kehl • kor • tuh*
I've locked myself out of my room.	**Jeg har låst meg ute fra rommet.** *yay hahr lawst may ew` • tuh fra rum´ • muh*
There's no hot water/toilet paper.	**Jeg har ikke varmt vann/toalettpapir.** *yay hahr ihk` • kuh vahrmt vahn/ tu • ah • leht´ • pah • peer*
The room is dirty.	**Rommet er skittent.** *rum´ • muh ar shiht` • tuhnt*
There are bugs in our room.	**Det er insekter på rommet vårt.** *deh ar ihn` • sehk • tuhr poh rum´ • muh vohrt*
…doesn't work.	**…virker ikke.** *…vihr` • kuhr ihk` • kuh*
Can you fix…?	**Kan du få fikset…?** *kahn dew faw fihk` • suht…*
the air conditioning	**klimaanlegget** *klee´ • mah • ahn • lehg • guh*
the fan	**viften** *vihf` • tuhn*

the heat [heating]	**varmen**
	vahr` • muhn
the light	**lyset**
	lui´s • uh
the TV	**TVen**
	teh` • veh • uhn
the toilet	**toalettet**
	tu • ah • _leht_´ • tuh
I'd like to move to another room.	**Jeg vil gjerne flytte til et annet rom.**
	yay vihl _ya_`r • nuh _fluit_` • tuh tihl eht _ahn_` • nuht rum

CHECKING OUT

When's check-out?	**Når må jeg sjekke ut?**
	nohr maw yay _shehk_` • kuh **ewt**
Could I leave my bags here until…?	**Kan jeg sette igjen bagasjen min til…?**
	kahn yay _seht_` • tuh ih • _yehn_´ bah • _gah_´ • shuhn mihn tihl…
Can I have an itemized bill/ a receipt?	**Kan jeg få en spesifisert regning/ kvittering?**
	kahn yay faw ehn speh • sih • fih • _sehrt_´ ray´ • ning/kviht • _teh_´ • rihng
I think there's a mistake in the bill.	**Jeg tror det er en feil på regningen.**
	yay _troo_r deh ar ehn fayl poh ray´ • ning • uhn
I'll pay in cash/by credit card.	**Jeg betaler kontant/med kredittkort.**
	yay buh • _tah_´ • luhr kun • _tahnt_´/meh kreh • diht´ • kohrt

RENTING

I've reserved an apartment/a room.	**Jeg har bestilt leilighet/rom.**
	yay hahr buh • _stihlt_´ _lay_` • li • _heht_/rum

My name is…	**Jeg heter…**
	yay <u>heh</u>` • tuhr…
Can I have the key/ key card?	**Kan jeg få nøkkelen/nøkkelkortet?**
	kahn yay faw <u>nurk</u>` • kuhl • uhn/ <u>nurk</u>` • kuhl • kor • tuh
Are there…?	**Fins det…?**
	fihns deh…
dishes	**servise**
	sehr • <u>vee</u>´ • suh
pillows	**puter**
	<u>pew</u>` • tuhr
sheets	**lakener**
	<u>lah</u>´ • kuhn • uhr
towels	**håndklær**
	<u>hohng</u>` • klar
When/Where do I put out the trash [rubbish] recycling?	**Når/Hvor setter jeg ut søppelet?**
	nohr/voor <u>seht</u>´ • tuhr yay ewt <u>surp</u>´ • puhl • uh
…is broken.	**…er gått i stykker.**
	…ar goht ih <u>stuik</u>´ • kuhr
How does…work?	**Hvordan virker…?**
	<u>voor</u>´ • dahn <u>vihr</u>` • kuhr

the air conditioner	**klimaanlegget**
	klee´ • mah • ahn • lehg • guh
the dishwasher	**oppvaskmaskinen**
	ohp` • vahsk • mah • sheen • uhn
the freezer	**fryseren**
	frui` • suhr • uhn
the heater	**varmeovnen**
	vahr` • muh • ohv • nuhn
the microwave	**mikrobølgeovnen**
	mih´ • kru • burl • guh • ohv • nuhn
the refrigerator	**kjøleskapet**
	khur • luh • skahpuh
the stove	**komfyren**
	kohm • _fui´_ • ruhn
the washing machine	**vaskemaskinen**
	vahs` • kuh • mah • sheen • uhn

DOMESTIC ITEMS

I need...	**Jeg trenger...**
	yay _trehng´_ • uhr...
an adapter	**en adapter**
	ehn ah • _dahp´_ • tuhr
aluminum [kitchen] foil	**aluminiumsfolie**
	ah • lew • _meen´_ • yewms • fool • yuh
a bottle opener	**en flaskeåpner**
	ehn _flahs`_ • kuh • awp • nuhr
a broom	**en feiekost**
	ehn _fay`_ • uh • kust
a can opener	**en boksåpner**
	ehn _bohks`_ • awp • nuhr
cleaning supplies	**rengjøringsmidler**
	rehn` • yurr • ihngs • mihd • luhr
a corkscrew	**en korketrekker**
	ehn _kohr`_ • kuh • trehk • kuhr

detergent	**vaskemiddel**
	vahs` • kuh • mihd • duhl
dish detergent	**oppvaskmiddel**
	ohp` • vahsk • mid • duhl
bin bags	**søppelsekker**
	surp` • puhl • sehk • kuhr
a light bulb	**en lyspære**
	ehn _lui`s_ • pa • ruh
matches	**fyrstikker**
	fuir` • stihk • kuhr
a mop	**en mopp**
	ehn mawp
a napkin	**en serviett**
	ehn sehrv • yeht´
paper towels	**husholdningspapir**
	hews • _hohl´_ • nihngs • pah • peer
plastic wrap	**plastfolie**
[cling film]	_plahst´_ • fool • yuh
a plunger	**en klosettpumpe**
	ehn klu • seht´ • pum • puh
scissors	**en saks**
	ehn sahks
a vacuum cleaner	**en støvsuger**
	ehn _stur`v_ • sewg • uhr

For In the Kitchen, see page 194.

AT THE HOSTEL

Do you have any places left for tonight?	**Har dere noen plasser ledig for i natt?**
	hahr d_eh_` • ruh n_oo_` • uhn plahs` • suhr _leh_` • dih fohr ih naht
Can I have…?	**Kan jeg få…?**
	kahn yay faw…

a single/double room	**et enkeltrom/dobbeltrom** *eht ehng´•kuhlt•rum/dohb´•buhlt•rum*
a blanket	**et ullteppe** *eht ewl`•tehp•puh*
a pillow	**en pute** *ehn pew`•tuh*
some sheets	**noe sengetøy** *nu•eh sehng•eh•tury*
soap	**såpe** *saw`•puh*
towels	**håndklær** *hohng`•klar*
What time do you lock up?	**Når stenges ytterdøra?** *nohr stehng`•uhs uit`•tuhr•dur•rah*

There are well over 100 hostels throughout Norway run by two different chains: Hostelling International, monitored by **Norske Vandrerhjem** (the Norwegian branch of Hostelling International), and VIP Backpackers Resorts International. Located in cities as well as natural settings like fjords and along the coast, hostels are an inexpensive option. In many cases you may request a private or shared room. The charge per night covers only the cost of the room. Sheets may be brought from home or rented, and meals are separate.

GOING CAMPING

Can we camp here?	**Kan vi campe her?** *kahn vee kehm`•puh har*
Is there a campsite nearby?	**Er det en campingplass i nærheten?** *ar deh ehn kehm´•pihng•plahs ih nar´•heh•tuhn*

What is the charge per day/week?	**Hva koster det per dag/uke?**
	vah <u>kohs</u>` • tuhr deh pehr dahg/<u>**ew**</u>` • kuh
Are there…?	**Fins det…?**
	fihns deh…
cooking facilities	**kokemuligheter**
	<u>koo</u>` • kuh • mew • lih • heht • uhr
electrical outlets	**innlagt strøm**
	<u>ihn</u>´ • lahkt strurm
laundry facilities	**vaskemuligheter**
	<u>vahs</u>` • kuh • mew • lih • heht • uhr
showers	**dusj**
	dewsh
tents for rent [hire]	**telt til leie**
	tehlt tihl <u>lay</u>` • uh
Where can I empty the chemical toilet?	**Hvor kan jeg tømme det kjemiske toalettet?**
	*voor kahn yay <u>turm</u>` • muh de <u>kh**eh**</u>´ • mihs • kuh tu • ah • <u>leht</u>´ • uh*

For In the Kitchen, see page 194.

YOU MAY SEE…

DRIKKEVANN	drinking water
CAMPING FORBUDT	no camping
BRUK AV ÅPEN ILD FORBUDT	no fires
GRILLING FORBUDT	no barbecues

COMMUNICATIONS

NEED TO KNOW

Where's an internet cafe?	**Hvor finner jeg en internettkafé?** *voor fihn´ • nuhr yay ehn ihn´ • tuhr • neht • kah • feh*
Can I access the internet/check e-mail?	**Kan jeg bruke internett/sjekke e-post?** *kahn yay brew` • kuh ihn´ • tuhr • neht/ shehk` • kuh eh´ • pohst*
How much per hour/ half hour?	**Hvor mye er det for en time/halv time?** *voor mui` • uh ar deh fohr ehn tee` • muh/hahl tee` • muh*
How do I connect/ log on?	**Hvordan kobler jeg meg opp/ logger jeg meg inn?** *voor´ • dahn kohb` • luhr yay may ohp/ lohg` • guhr yay may ihn*
Can I have a phone card?	**Kan jeg få et telefonkort?** *kahn yay faw eht teh • luh • foon´ • kohrt*
Can I have your phone number?	**Kan jeg få telefonnummeret ditt?** *kahn yay faw teh • luh • foon´ • num • muhr • uh diht*
Here's my number/ e-mail address.	**Her har du nummeret mitt/ e-postadressen min.** *har hahr dew num´ • muhr • uh miht/ eh´ • pohst • ahd • rehs • suhn mihn*
Call me.	**Ring meg.** *rihng may*
E-mail me.	**Send meg en e-post.** *sehn may ehn eh´ • pohst*
Hello. This is…	**Hallo. Dette er…** *hah • loo´ deht` • tuh ar…*

I'd like to speak to…	**Kan jeg få snakke med…?**
	kahn yay faw <u>snahk`</u> • kuh meh…
Can you repeat that?	**Kan du gjenta det?**
	kahn dew <u>yehn´</u> • tah deh
I'll call back later.	**Jeg ringer igjen senere.**
	yay <u>rihng´</u> • uhr ih • <u>yehn´</u> <u>seh`</u> • nuh • ruh
Goodbye.	**Adjø.**
	ahd • <u>yur´</u>
Where's the post office?	**Hvor er postkontoret?**
	voor ar <u>pohst`</u> • kun • toor • uh
Can I send this to…?	**Kan jeg få sendt dette til…?**
	kahn yay faw sehnt <u>deht`</u> • tuh tihl…

ONLINE

Where's an internet cafe?	**Hvor finner jeg en internettkafé?**
	voor <u>fihn´</u> • nuhr yay ehn <u>ihn´</u> • tuhr • neht • kah • feh
Does it have wireless internet?	**Har den trådløst internett?**
	<u>hah</u>r dehn <u>traw`</u> • lurst <u>ihn´</u> • tuhr • neht

What is the WiFi password?	**Hva er WiFi-passordet?**
	vah ar vee • fee • pahs • ur • eht
Is the WiFi free?	**Er WiFi gratis?**
	ar vee • fee grah • tihs
Do you have bluetooth?	**Har dere bluetooth?**
	hahr dehr • eh blew • tewth
How do I turn the computer on/off?	**Hvordan slår jeg på/av datamaskinen?**
	<u>voor</u>´ • dahn slawr yay p<u>aw</u>/ah
	<u>dah</u>´ • tah • mah • sheen • uhn
Can I...?	**Kan jeg...?**
	kahn yay...
access the Internet	**bruke internett**
	<u>brew</u>` • kuh <u>ihn</u>´ • tuhr • neht
check e-mail	**sjekke e-post**
	<u>shehk</u>` • kuh <u>eh</u>´ • pohst
print	**skrive ut**
	skree` • vuh <u>ewt</u>
plug in/charge my laptop/iPhone/ iPad/BlackBerry	**koble til/lade min bærbare maskin/ iPhone/iPad? BlackBerry**
	kawb` • leh tihl/lah • deh mihn bar • bahr • eh mah • sheen/ay • foan/ ay • pad/blahk • behr • ree
access Skype	**bruke Skype**
	brew • keh skayp

How much per hour/ half hour?	**Hvor mye er det for en time/halv time?**
	voor <u>mui</u>` • uh <u>a</u>r deh fohr ehn <u>tee</u>` • muh/ hahl <u>tee</u>` • muh
How do I...?	**Hvordan...?**
	<u>voor</u>´ • dahn...
connect/ disconnect	**kobler jeg meg opp/fra**
	<u>kohb</u>` • luhr yay may ohp/fr<u>ah</u>
log on/off	**logger jeg meg inn/ut**
	<u>lohg</u>` • guhr jay may ihn/<u>ewt</u>
type this symbol	**skriver jeg dette tegnet**
	<u>skree</u>` • vuhr yay <u>deht</u>` • tuh tay´ • nuh
What's your e-mail?	**Hva er e-postadressen din?**
	vah ar <u>eh</u>´ • pohst • ahd • rehs • suhn dihn

YOU MAY SEE... 👁

LUKK	close
SLETT	delete
E-POST	e-mail
AVSLUTT	exit
HJELP	help
INSTANT MESSENGER	instant messenger
INTERNETT	internet
PÅLOGGING	log in
NY (MELDING)	new (message)
PÅ/AV	on/off
ÅPNE	open
SKRIV UT	print
LAGRE	save
SEND	send
BRUKERNAVN/PASSORD	username/password
TRÅDLØST INTERNETT	wireless internet

My e-mail is…	**E-postadressen min er…**
	eh´ • pohst • ahd • rehs • suhn mihn ar…
Do you have a scanner?	**Har dere en skanner?**
	hahr dehr • eh ehn skahn • ehr

SOCIAL MEDIA

Are you on Facebook/ Twitter?	**Er du på Facebook/Twitter?**
	ar dew paw feis • bewk/ tviht • ehr
What's your user name?	**Hva er brukernavnet ditt?**
	vah ar brewk • ehr • nahvn • eht diht
I'll add you as a friend.	**Jeg legger deg til som venn.**
	yay lehg • ehr day tihl sawm vehn
I'll follow you on Twitter.	**Jeg følger deg på Twitter.**
	yay furl • ehr day paw tviht • ehr
Are you following…?	**Følger du…?**
	furl • her dew
I'll put the pictures on Facebook/ Twitter.	**Jeg legger ut bildene på Facebook/ Twitter.**
	yay lehg • ehr ewt bihl • deh • neh paw feis • bewk/tviht • ehr
I'll tag you in the pictures.	**Jeg tagger deg i bildene.**
	yay tag • ehr day ee bihl • dehn • eh

PHONE

In Norway, public phones accept coins, credit cards or **telekort** (prepaid phone cards), which are available at most kiosks, post offices and major train stations.
To call the U.S. or Canada from Norway, dial 00 + 1 + area code + phone number. To call the U.K., dial 00 + 44 + area code (minus the first 0) + phone number. Useful numbers include: information **1880**; operator assistance **1882**.

Can I have a phone card/prepaid calling time for... crowns?	**Kan jeg få et telefonkort/ringetid for... kroner?**
	kahn yay faw eht teh • luh • foon´ • kohrt/ rihng` • uh • teed fohr...kroo`n • uhr
How much?	**Hvor mye koster det?**
	voor mui` • uh kohs` • tuhr deh
Where's the pay phone?	**Hvor er telefonautomaten?**
	voor ar teh • leh • fun • ev • tu • maht • ehn
What's the area/ country code for...?	**Hva er retningsnummeret/landkoden til...?**
	vah ar reht` • nihngs • num • muhr • uh/ lahn` • kood • uhn tihl...
What's the number for Information?	**Hva er nummeret til Opplysningen?**
	vah ar num´ • muhr • uh tihl ohp • luis´ • nihng • uhn
Can I have the number for...?	**Kan jeg få nummeret til...?**
	kahn yay faw num´ • muhr • uh tihl...
I'd like to call collect [reverse the charges].	**Jeg vil ringe med noteringsoverføring [mottaker betaler].**
	yay vihl rihn • geh meh nut • ehr • ihngs • awv • ehr • furr • ihng mut • ahk • ehr beh • tah • lehr
My cell [mobile] phone doesn't work here.	**Mobilen min virker ikke her.**
	mu • beel´ • uhn mihn vihr` • kuhr ihk` • kuh har

What network are you on?	**Hvilket nettverk er du på?**
	vihl • keht neht • vahrk ar dew paw
Is it 3G?	**Er det 3G?**
	ar deh treh • geh
I have run out of credit/minutes.	**Jeg gikk tom for kreditt/minutter.**
	yay yihk tawm fawr kreh • diht/ mihn • ewt • ehr
Can I buy some credit?	**Kan jeg kjøpe litt kreditt?**
	kahn yay shur • peh liht kreh • diht
Do you have a phone charger?	**Har du en telefonlader?**
	hahr dew ehn teh • leh • fun • lah • dehr
Can I have your number?	**Kan jeg få nummeret ditt?**
	kahn yay faw <u>num´</u> • muhr • uh diht
My number is…	**Nummeret mitt er…**
	<u>num´</u> • muhr • uh miht ar…
Can you call me?	**Kan du ringe meg?**
	kahn dew <u>rihng`</u> • uh may
Can you text me?	**Kan du sende meg en tekstmelding?**
	kahn dew <u>sehn`</u> • nuh may ehn <u>tehkst´</u> • mehl • lihng
I'll call you.	**Jeg ringer deg.**
	yay <u>rihng`</u> • uhr day
I'll text you.	**Jeg sender deg en tekstmelding.**
	yay <u>sehn`</u> • nuhr day ehn <u>tehkst´</u> • mehl • lihng

YOU MAY HEAR...

Hvem er det som ringer?	Who's calling?
vehm <u>ar</u> deh sohm <u>rihng</u>` • uhr	
Et øyeblikk.	Hold on.
eht <u>ury</u>` • uh • blihk	
Jeg skal sette deg over.	I'll put you
yay skahl <u>seht</u>` • tuh day <u>aw</u>´ • vuhr	through.
Han/Hun er ute for øyeblikket.	He's/She's out
hahn/hewn ar <u>ew</u>` • tuh fohr	at the moment.
<u>ury</u>` • uh • blihk • kuh	
Han/Hun kan ikke ta telefonen	He/She can't
akkurat nå.	come to the
hahn/hewn kahn <u>ihk</u>` • kuh tah	phone right now.
teh • luh • <u>foon</u>´ • uhn <u>ahk</u>´ • kew • raht naw	
Vil du legge igjen en beskjed?	Would you like to
vihl dew <u>lehg</u>` • guh ih • <u>yehn</u>´	leave a
ehn buh • sheh´	message?
Ring igjen senere/om ti minutter.	Call back later/
rihng ih • <u>yehn</u>´ <u>seh</u>` • nuh • ruh/ohm t<u>ee</u>	in 10 minutes.
mihn • <u>ewt</u>´ • tuhr	
Kan han/hun ringe deg opp?	Can he/she call
kahn hahn/ hewn <u>rihng</u>` • uh day ohp	you back?
Hva er nummeret ditt?	What's your
vah ar <u>num</u>´ • muh • ruh diht	number?

PHONE ETIQUETTE

Hello. This is...	**Hallo. Dette er...**
	hah • <u>loo</u>´ <u>deht</u>` • tuh ar...
Can I speak to...?	**Kan jeg få snakke med...?**
	kahn yay faw <u>snahk</u>` • kuh meh...

Extension…	**Linje…** *lihn` • yuh…*
Can you speak louder/ more slowly?	**Kan du snakke litt høyere/ langsommere?** *kahn dew snahk` • kuh liht hury` • uhr • uh/ lahng` • sohm • muhr • uh*
Can you repeat that?	**Kan du gjenta det?** *kahn dew yehn´ • tah deh*
I'll call back later.	**Jeg ringer igjen senere.** *yay rihng` • uhr ih • yehn´ seh` • nuh • ruh*
Goodbye.	**Adjø.** *ahd • yur´*

FAX

Can I send/receive a fax here?	**Kan jeg sende/motta faks her?** *kahn yay sehn` • nuh/ moot´ • tah fahks har*
What's the fax number?	**Hva er faksnummeret?** *vah ar fahks´ • num • muh • ruh*
Please fax this to…	**Kan du fakse dette til…** *kahn dew fahks` • uh deht` • tuh tihl…*

POST

Where's the post office/mailbox [postbox]?	**Hvor finner jeg et postkontor/en postkasse?** *voor fihn´ • nuhr yay eht pohst´ • kun • toor/ ehn pohst´ • kahs • suh*
A stamp for this letter/postcard, please.	**Et frimerke til dette brevet/kortet, takk.** *eht free´ • mehrk • uh til deht` • tuh breh´ • vuh/kohr´ • tuh tahk*
How much?	**Hvor mye koster det?** *voor mui´ • uh kohs` • tuhr deh*

I'd like to send this by airmail/express mail.	**Jeg vil gjerne sende dette med flypost/ ekspress.**
	yay vihl <u>ya `r</u> • nuh <u>sehn`</u> • nuh <u>deht`</u> • tuh meh flui • <u>pohst</u>/ehks • <u>prehs´</u>
Can I have a receipt?	**Kan jeg få kvittering?**
	kahn yay faw kviht • <u>teh´</u> • rihng

Norwegian post offices are generally open Monday to Friday from 8:00 a.m. to 4:00 p.m. and Saturday from 9:00 a.m. to 1:00 p.m. Mailboxes are painted red and display the trumpet symbol of the post office.

YOU MAY HEAR...

Kan du fylle ut en tolldeklarasjon?	Can you fill out
kahn dew <u>fuil`</u> • luh ewt ehn	the customs
<u>*tohl`*</u> *• deh • klah • rah • shoon*	declaration form?
Hva er verdien?	What's the
vah ar vehr • <u>dee´</u> • uhn	value?
Hva er det inni?	What's inside?
vah <u>ar</u> deh <u>ihn`</u> • ih	

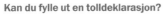

SIGHTSEEING

NEED TO KNOW

Where's the tourist information office?	**Hvor er turistkontoret?** *voor ar tew • rihst´ • kun • too • ruh*
What are the main points of interest?	**Hva er de viktigste severdighetene?** *vah ar dih vihk` • tik • stuh seh • vehr´ • dih • heh • tuh • nuh*
Do you have tours in English?	**Har dere omvisninger på engelsk?** *hahr deh` • ruh ohm´ • vihs • nihng • uhr poh ehng´ • uhlsk*
Can I have a map/ guide?	**Kan jeg få et kart/en guide?** *kahn yay faw eht kahrt/ehn gied*

TOURIST INFORMATION

Do you have any information on...?	**Har dere informasjon om...?** *hahr deh` • ruh ihn • fohr • mah • shoo´n ohm...*
Can you recommend...?	**Kan dere anbefale...?** *kahn deh` • ruh ahn´ • buh • fah • luh...*
a boat trip	**en båttur** *ehn bawt` • tewr*
an excursion	**en utflukt** *ehn ew`t • flewkt*
a sightseeing tour	**en sightseeingtur** *ehn siet´ • see • ihng • tewr*

For Asking Directions, see page 64.

Tourist offices are located throughout Norway. The local tourist office can provide information for visitors on accommodation, activities and other entertainment. Visit Norway, the official website of the Norwegian Tourist Board, www.visitnorway.com, can provide information about locations in particular cities.

ON TOUR

I'd like to go on the tour to...	**Jeg vil gjerne bli med på turen til...** _yay vihl <u>ya`r</u> • nuh blih meh poh <u>tew´</u> • ruhn tihl..._
When's the next tour?	**Når går neste tur?** _nohr gawr <u>nehs`</u> • tuh tewr_
Are there tours in English?	**Fins det turer på engelsk?** _fihns deh <u>tew`r</u> • uhr poh <u>ehng´</u> • uhlsk_
Is there an English-speaking guide/an audio guide in English?	**Fins det en engelsktalende guide/en lydguide på engelsk?** _fihns deh ehn <u>ehng´</u> • uhlsk • <u>tahl</u> • uhn • uh gied/ehn <u>luid`</u> • gied poh <u>ehng´</u> • uhlsk_
What time do we leave?	**Når drar vi?** _nohr drahr vee_

What time do we return?	**Når kommer vi tilbake?**
	nohr kohm´ • muhr vee tihl • bah` • kuh
We'd like to see...	**Vi vil gjerne se på...**
	vee vihl ya`r • nuh seh poh...
Can we stop here...?	**Kan vi stoppe her...?**
	kahn vee stohp` • puh har...
to take photographs	**for å ta bilder**
	fohr oh tah bihl` • duhr
to buy souvenirs	**for å kjøpe suvenirer**
	fohr oh khur` • puh sew • vuh • nee´r • uhr
to use the restroom [toilet]	**for å gå på toalettet**
	forh oh gaw poh tu • ah • leh´ • tuh
Is it disabled-accessible?	**Er det adkomst for bevegelseshemmede?**
	ar deh ahd` • kohmst fohr buh • veh´ • guhl • suhs • hem • muhd • uh

For Tickets, see page 45.

SEEING THE SIGHTS

Where is/are...?	**Hvor er...?**
	voor ar...
the battleground	**slagstedet**
	slah`g • steh • duh
the botanical gardens	**den botaniske hagen**
	dehn bu • tah´ • nihsk • uh hah` • guhn
the castle	**slottet**
	slot´ • tuh
the downtown area	**sentrum**
	sehn´ • trewm
the fair	**markedet**
	mahr` • kehd • uh
the fortress	**festningen**
	fehst` • nihng • uhn

the fountain	**fontenen**	
	fon • <u>teh</u>` • nuhn	
the library	**biblioteket**	
	bihb • lyu • <u>teh</u>´ • kuh	
the market	**torget**	
	<u>tohr</u>´ • guh	
the museum	**museet**	
	mew • <u>seh</u>´ • uh	
the old town	**gamlebyen**	
	<u>gahm</u>` • luh • bui • uhn	
the palace	**slottet**	
	<u>slot</u>´ • tuh	
the park	**parken**	
	<u>pahr</u>´ • kuhn	
the ruins	**ruinene**	
	rew • <u>ee</u>´n • uh • nuh	
the shopping area	**handlestrøket**	
	<u>hahn</u>`d • luh • str<u>ur</u> • kuh	
the town square	**rådhusplassen**	
	<u>rawd</u>` • <u>hews</u> • plah • suhn	
Can you show me on the map?	**Kan du vise meg på kartet hvor jeg er?**	
	*kahn dew <u>vee</u>` • suh may paw <u>kahr</u>´ • tuh voor yay **ar***	

It's...	**Det er...**
	*deh **ar**...*
amazing	**praktfullt**
	prahkt` • fewlt
beautiful	**vakkert**
	vahk´ • kuhrt
boring	**kjedelig**
	kheh` • duh • lih
interesting	**interessant**
	ihn • tuh • rehs • sahng´t
magnificent	**storslagent**
	stoo`r • slahg • uhnt
romantic	**romantisk**
	ru • mahn´ • tihsk
strange	**underlig**
	ewn` • dur • lih
stunning	**overveldende**
	aw` • vuhr • vehl • duhn • uh
terrible	**forferdelig**
	fohr • fa´r • duh • lih
ugly	**stygt**
	stuikt
I (don't) like it.	**Jeg liker det (ikke).**
	yay lee´ • kuhr deh (ihk` • kuh)

RELIGIOUS SITES

Where's...?	**Hvor er...?**
	*voor **ar**...*
the cathedral	**domkirken**
	<u>dohm</u>´ • khihr • kuhn
the church	**kirken**
	<u>khihr</u>` • kuhn
the mosque	**moskéen**
	mus • <u>keh</u>´ • uhn
the synagogue	**synagogen**
	sui • nah • <u>goo</u>` • guhn
the temple	**templet**
	<u>tehm</u>´p • luh
What time is mass/ the service?	**Når begynner messen/gudstjenesten?**
	*nohr buh • <u>yuin</u>´ • nuhr <u>mehs</u>` • suhn/ <u>gewds</u>´ • ty**eh** • nuhs • tuhn*

ACTIVITIES

SHOPPING

NEED TO KNOW

Where is the market/ mall [shopping centre]?	**Hvor er torget/kjøpesenteret?** *voor ar <u>tohr´</u> • guh/ <u>khur`</u> • puh • sehn • truh*
I'm just looking.	**Jeg bare ser meg omkring.** *yay <u>bah`</u> • ruh sehr may ohm • <u>krihng´</u>*
Can you help me?	**Kan du hjelpe meg?** *kahn dew <u>yehl`</u> • puh may*
I'm being helped.	**Jeg får hjelp.** *yay fawr yehlp*
How much?	**Hvor mye koster det?** *voor <u>mew`</u> • uh <u>kohs`</u> • tuhr deh*
That one.	**Den der.** *dehn dar*
No, thanks. That's all.	**Nei takk. Det var alt.** *nay tahk deh vahr ahlt*
Where do I pay?	**Hvor betaler man?** *voor buh • <u>tah´</u> • luhr mahn*
I'll pay in cash/by credit card.	**Jeg betaler kontant/med kredittkort.** *yay buh • <u>tah´</u> • luhr kun • <u>tahn´t</u>/meh kreh • <u>diht´</u> • kohrt*
Could I have a receipt?	**Kan jeg få kvittering?** *kahn yay faw kviht • <u>teh´</u> • rihng*

YOU MAY SEE...

UTE TIL LUNSJ	closed for lunch
BETAL HER	pay here
VI TAR KREDITTKORT	credit cards accepted
ÅPNINGSTIDER	opening hours

AT THE SHOPS

Norway offers shopping choices for a range of budgets. Even in the capital, a good deal of shopping can be done on foot. Many of the major stores are located in the area around **Karl Johans** gate and on **Bogstadveien** and **Hegdehaugsveien** streets. **Grünerløkka** is the place to go to find trendy boutiques showcasing the work of young Norwegian designers. Here you'll also find lots of second-hand shops, music stores and independent stores selling local pottery and handicrafts. For everything under one roof in Oslo, visit **Aker Brygge**, **Byporten**, **Glasmagasinet**, **Oslo City**, **Paleet**, **Steen & Strøm** and **Vikaterrassen**. Regular store hours are Monday to Friday from 9:00 a.m. to 5:00 p.m. (on Saturday to 3:00 p.m.), but many stores stay open later. Shopping malls are generally open Monday to Friday from 10:00 a.m. to 9:00 p.m. and Saturday from 9:00 a.m. to 6:00 p.m. Most stores are closed on Sunday.

Where is...?	**Hvor er det...?**
	voor ar deh...
the antiques store	**en antikvitetshandel**
	ehn ahn•tih•kvih•teh´ts•hahn•duhl
the bakery	**et bakeri**
	eht bah•kuhr•ee´

the bank	**en bank**
	ehn bahngk
the bookstore	**en bokhandel**
	ehn book`•hahn•duhl
the clothing store	**en klesbutikk**
	ehn kleh`s•bew•tihk
the delicatessen	**en delikatesseforretning**
	ehn deh•lih•kah•tehs´•suh•fohr•reht•nihng
the department store	**et stormagasin**
	eht stoor`•mah•gah•seen
the gift shop	**en gavebutikk**
	ehn gah`•vuh•bew•tihk
the health food store	**en helsekostbutikk**
	ehn hehl`•suh•kohst•fohr•reht•nihng
the jeweler	**en gullsmed**
	ehn gewl`•smeh
the liquor store [off-licence]	**et vinmonopol**
	eht vee`n•mu•nu•pool
the market	**et torg**
	eht tohrg
the music store	**musikkforretningen**
	mews•ihk•fawr•eht•nihng•ehn
the pastry shop	**et konditori**
	eht kun•dih•tu•ree´
the pharmacy [chemist]	**et apotek**
	eht ah•pu•teh´k
the produce [grocery] store	**en matvarebutikk**
	ehn mah`t•vah•ruh•bew•tihk
the shoe store	**en skoforretning**
	ehn skoo´•fohr•reht´•nihng
the shopping mall	**et butikksenter**
	eht bew•tihk´•sehn•tuhr
the souvenir store	**en suvenirbutikk**
	ehn sew•vuh•nee´r•bew•tihk

Where is...?	**Hvor er det...?**
	voor ar deh...
the supermarket	**et supermarked**
	eht <u>sew´</u> • puhr • mahr • kuhd
the tobacconist	**en tobakksbutikk**
	ehn tu • <u>bahk´s</u> • bew • tihk
the toy store	**en leketøysbutikk**
	ehn <u>leh`</u> • kuh • turys • bew • tihk

YOU MAY HEAR...

Kan jeg hjelpe deg?	Can I help you?
kahn yay <u>yehl`</u> • puh day	
Et øyeblikk.	One moment.
eht <u>ury`</u> • uh • blihk	
Hva skal det være?	What would you
vah skahl deh <u>va`</u> • ruh	like?
Skal det være noe annet?	Anything else?
skahl deh <u>va`</u> • ruh <u>noo`</u> • uh <u>ahn`</u> • nuht	

ASK AN ASSISTANT

When do you open/close?	**Når åpner/stenger dere?**
	nawr åwpn • er/stehng • ehr dehr • eh
When does... open/close?	**Når åpner/stenger...?**
	nohr <u>aw`</u>p • nuhr/<u>stehng`</u> • uhr...
Where is...?	**Hvor er...?**
	voor ar...
the cash desk	**kassen**
	<u>kahs`</u> • suhn
the escalator	**rulletrappen**
	<u>rewl`</u> • luh • trahp • puhn

the elevator [lift]	**heisen**	
	hay´ • suhn	
the fitting room	**prøverommet**	
	prur` • vuh • rum • muh	
the store directory [guide]	**butikkguiden**	
	bew • _tihk´_ • gie • duhn	
Can you help me?	**Kan du hjelpe meg?**	
	kahn dew _yehl`_ • puh may	
I'm just looking.	**Jeg bare ser meg omkring.**	
	yay _bah´_ • ruh sehr may ohm • _krihng´_	
I'm being helped.	**Jeg får hjelp.**	
	yay fawr yehlp	
Do you have anything in…?	**Har du noe i…?**	
	hahr dew _noo`_ • uh ih…	
Can you show me…?	**Kan du vise meg…?**	
	kahn dew _vee`_ • suh may…	
Can you ship/ wrap it?	**Kan du sende den/pakke den inn?**	
	kahn dew _seh`_ • nuh dehn/_pahk`_ • kuh dehn ihn	
How much?	**Hvor mye koster det?**	
	voor _mui`_ • uh _kohs`_ • tuhr deh	
That's all.	**Det var alt.**	
	deh var ahlt	

For Souvenirs, see page 121.

PERSONAL PREFERENCES

I'd like something…	**Jeg vil gjerne ha noe…**	
	yay vihl _ya`r_ • nuh hah _noo`_ • uh…	
cheap/expensive	**billig/dyrt**	
	bihl • lih/_dui_rt	
larger/smaller	**større/mindre**	
	sturr´ • ruh/_mihn´_ • druh	

from this region	**fra dette området**
	frah <u>deht`</u> *• tuh* <u>ohm`</u> *• raw • duh*
Is it real?	**Er den ekte?**
	ar dehn <u>ehk`</u> *• tuh*
Could you show me this/that?	**Kan du vise meg den/den der?**
	kahn dew <u>vee`</u> *• suh may dehn/dehn dar*
It's not quite what I want.	**Det var ikke akkurat det jeg hadde tenkt meg.**
	deh vahr <u>ihk`</u> *• kuh* <u>ahk`</u> *• kew • räht deh yay* <u>hahd`</u> *• duh tehngkt may*
No, I don't like it.	**Nei, jeg liker det ikke.**
	nay yay <u>lee´</u> *• kuhr deh* <u>ihk`</u> *• kuh*
That's too expensive.	**Det er for dyrt.**
	deh ar fohr duirt
I'd like to think about it.	**Jeg må tenke på det.**
	yay moh <u>tehng`</u> *• kuh poh deh*
I'll take it.	**Jeg tar det.**
	yay tahr deh

Major credit cards are accepted at most hotels, restaurants, large shops, car rental companies and airlines, though some places will not accept them, particularly supermarkets and gas stations. It is a good idea to have some cash on hand, just in case. Traveler's checks are a safe alternative to cash, especially if you do not have a credit card.

PAYING & BARGAINING

How much?	**Hvor mye koster det?**
	voor <u>mui`</u> *• uh* <u>kohs`</u> *• tuhr deh*
I'll pay...	**Jeg betaler...**
	yay buh • <u>tah´</u> *• luhr...*

in cash	**kontant**
	kun • <u>tahn</u>´t
by credit card	**med kredittkort**
	meh kreh • <u>diht</u>´ • kohrt
by traveler's	**med reisesjekk**
check [cheque]	*meh <u>ray</u>` • suh • shehk*
Could I have	**Kan jeg få kvittering?**
a receipt?	*kahn yay faw kviht • <u>teh</u>´ • rihng*
That's too much.	**Det er for mye.**
	deh ar fohr <u>mew</u>` • uh
I'll give you...	**Jeg gir deg...**
	yay yeer day...
I only have...kroner.	**Jeg har bare...kroner.**
	yay hahr <u>bah</u>` • ruh... <u>kroo</u>` • nuhr
Is that your best	**Er det ditt siste tilbud?**
price?	*ar deh diht <u>sihs</u>` • tuh <u>tihl</u>` • bewd*
Can you give me	**Kan du gi meg avslag?**
a discount?	*kahn dew yee may <u>ahv</u>` • slahg*

For Numbers, see page 22.

YOU MAY HEAR...

Hvordan vil du betale?
<u>voor´</u>•dahn vihl dew buh•<u>tah´</u>•luh

How are you paying?

Kredittkortet ditt ble avslått.
kreh•diht•kurt•eht diht bleh ahv•slawt

Your credit card has been declined.

ID, takk.
ee•deh tahk

ID, please.

Vi tar ikke kredittkort.
vee tahr ihke kreh•diht•kurt

We don't accept credit cards.

Kun kontant, takk.
kewn kun•tahnt tahk

Cash only, please.

Har du mindre sedler?
<u>hahr</u> dew <u>mihn´</u>•druh <u>sehd´</u>•luhr

Do you have any smaller change?

MAKING A COMPLAINT

I'd like...	**Jeg vil gjerne...** *yay vihl <u>ya`r</u>•nuh...*
to exchange this	**bytte dette** *<u>buit`</u>•tuh <u>deht`</u>•tuh*
to return this	**levere dette tilbake** *leh•<u>veh´</u>•ruh <u>deht`</u>•tuh tihl•<u>bah`</u>•kuh*
a refund	**ha pengene tilbake** *hah <u>pehng`</u>•uh•nuh tihl•<u>bah`</u>•kuh*
to see the manager	**snakke med butikksjefen** *<u>snahk`</u>•kuh meh buw•<u>tihk´</u>•shehf•uhn*

SERVICES

Can you recommend...?	**Kan du anbefale...?** *kahn dew <u>ahn´</u>•buh•fah•luh...*

a barber	**en herrefrisør**
	ehn hehr` • ruh • frih • surr
a dry cleaner	**et renseri**
	eht rehn • suh • ree´
a hairdresser	**en frisørsalong**
	ehn frih • sur´r • sah • lohng
a laundromat	**et vaskeri**
[launderette]	*eht vahs • kuh • ree´*
a nail salon	**en neglesalong**
	ehn nay` • luh • sah • lohng
a spa	**et spa**
	eht spah
a travel agency	**et reisebyrå**
	eht ray` • suh • bui • raw
Can you… this?	**Kan du…denne/dette?**
	kahn dew…dehn` • nuh/deht` • tuh
alter	**sy om**
	sui ohm
clean	**rense**
	rehn` • suh
mend	**lappe**
	lah` • puh
press	**presse**
	prehs` • suh
When will it be ready?	**Når er den/det ferdig?**
	nohr ar dehn/deh fa`r • dih

HAIR & BEAUTY

I'd like…	**Jeg vil gjerne ha…**
	yay vihl ya`r • nuh hah…
an appointment for today/ tomorrow	**en time i dag/i morgen**
	ehn tee` • muh ih dahg/ih maw` • ruhn

I'd like…	**Jeg vil gjerne ha…**
	yay vihl <u>ya`</u>•r • nuh hah…
an eyebrow/ bikini wax	**voksing av øyenbrynene/bikinilinjen**
	<u>vohk`</u> • sihng ah
	<u>ury`</u> • uhn • bruin • uh • nuh/
	bih • <u>kee´</u> • nih • lihn • yuhn
a facial	**en ansiktsbehandling**
	ehn <u>ahn`</u> • sihkts • buh • hahnd • lihng
a manicure/ pedicure	**manikyr/fotpleie**
	mah • nih • <u>kui´</u>r/<u>foot`</u> • play • uh
a massage	**massasje**
	mahs • <u>sah`</u> • shuh
some color	**litt farge**
	liht <u>fahr`</u> • guh
some highlights	**noen striper**
	<u>noo`</u> • uhn <u>stree`</u> • puhr
my hair styled	**håret stylet**
	<u>haw´</u> • ruh <u>stiel`</u> • uht
a hair cut	**en klipp**
	ehn klihp
a trim	**en stuss**
	ehn stews
Don't cut it too short.	**Klipp det ikke for kort.**
	klip deh <u>ihk`</u> • kuh fohr kohrt
Shorter here.	**Kortere her.**
	<u>kohr`</u> • tuhr • uh har
Do you do…?	**Tilbyr dere…?**
	<u>tihl´</u> • buir <u>deh`</u> • ruh…
acupuncture	**akupunktur**
	ah • kew • pewngk • <u>tew´</u>r
aromatherapy	**aromaterapi**
	ah • <u>roo´</u> • mah • teh • rah • pee
oxygen treatment	**surstoffbehandling**
	<u>sew`</u>r • stohf • buh • hahnd • lihng
Is there a sauna?	**Fins det sauna?**
	fihns deh <u>sev´</u> • nah

Many luxury hotels in Norway offer spa and other health and beauty treatments. **Geilo** (www.geilo.no) is a popular health and wellness retreat where you can also enjoy excellent skiing.

ANTIQUES

How old is this?	**Hvor gammel er den?** *voor <u>gahm</u> • muhl ar dehn*
Do you have anything of the...era?	**Har du noe fra...tiden?** *hahr dew <u>noo</u>` • uh fra... <u>tee</u>´ • duhn*
Do I have to fill out any forms?	**Må jeg fylle ut noen skjemaer?** *maw yay fyll • eh ewt nu • ehn sheh • mah • ehr*
Will I have problems with customs?	**Tror du jeg kan få problemer i tollen?** *troor dew yay kahn faw pru • <u>bleh</u>´ • muhr ih <u>tohl</u>´ • luhn*
Is there a certificate of authenticity?	**Har du et ekthetssertifikat?** *hahr dew et <u>ehkt</u>´ • <u>heh</u>ts • ser • tih • fih • kat*
Can you ship/ wrap it?	**Kan du sende den/pakke den inn?** *kahn dew <u>seh</u>` • nuh dehn/<u>pahk</u>` • kuh dehn ihn*

CLOTHING

I'd like...	**Jeg vil gjerne...** *yay vihl <u>yar</u>` • nuh...*
Can I try this on?	**Kan jeg prøve den?** *kahn yay <u>prur</u>` • vuh dehn*
It doesn't fit.	**Den passer ikke.** *dehn <u>pahs</u>` • suhr <u>ihk</u>` • kuh*

It's too...	**Den er for...**
	dehn ar fohr...
big/small	**stor/liten**
	lee´•tuhn/ stoor
short/long	**kort/lang**
	kohrt/lahng
tight/loose	**trang/stor**
	trahng/stur
Do you have this in size...?	**Har du denne i størrelse...?**
	hahr dew dehn`•nuh ih sturr`•rehl•suh...
Do you have this... in a bigger/ smaller size?	**Har du denne... i større/mindre størrelse?**
	hahr dew dehn`•nuh... ih sturr´•ruh/ mihn´•druh sturr•rehl•suh

For Numbers, see page 22.

YOU MAY HEAR...

Den kledde deg veldig godt.	That looks great on you.
dehn klehd•eh day vehl•dihg gawt	
Hvordan passer den?	How does it fit?
voor•dahn pahs•ehr dehn	
Vi har ikke din størrelse.	We don't have your size.
vee hahr ihk•eh dihn sturr•als•eh	

COLORS

I'd like something in...	**Jeg vil gjerne ha noe i...**
	yay vihl yar`•nuh hah noo`•uh ih...
beige	**beige**
	behsh

black	**svart**	
	svahrt	
blue	**blått**	
	bloht	
brown	**brunt**	
	brewnt	
gray	**grått**	
	groht	
green	**grønt**	
	grurnt	
orange	**oransje**	
	u • <u>rahng´</u> • shuh	
pink	**rosa**	
	<u>roo´</u> • sah	
purple	**fiolett**	
	fih • u • <u>leht´</u>	
red	**rødt**	
	rurt	
white	**hvitt**	
	viht	
yellow	**gult**	
	gewlt	

CLOTHES & ACCESSORIES

backpack	**en ryggsekk**
	ehn ruig` • sehk
belt	**et belte**
	eht behl` • tuh
bikini	**en bikini**
	ehn bih • kee´ • nih
blouse	**en bluse**
	ehn blew` • suh
bra	**en behå**
	ehn beh` • haw
briefs [underpants]	**en underbukse**
	ehn ewn` • uhr • buk • suh
coat	**en frakk** *m*/**kåpe** *f*
	ehn frahk/kaw` • puh
dress	**en kjole**
	ehn khoo` • luh
hat	**en hatt**
	ehn haht
jacket	**en jakke**
	ehn yahk` • kuh
jeans	**en olabukse**
	ehn oo` • lah • buk • suh
pajamas	**en pyjamas**
	ehn pui • shah´ • mahs
pants [trousers]	**en langbukse**
	ehn lahng` • buk • suh
panties (for women's underwear)	**undertøy**
	ewnd • ar • tury
panty hose [tights]	**en strømpebukse**
	ehn strurm` • puh • buk • suh
purse [handbag]	**en håndveske**
	ehn hohn` • vehs • kuh

raincoat	**en regnfrakk**
	ehn <u>rayn`</u> • frahk
scarf	**et skjerf**
	eht shehrf
shirt	**en skjorte**
	ehn <u>shoor`</u> • tuh
shorts	**et par shorts**
	eht pahr shawrts
skirt	**et skjørt**
	eht shurrt
socks	**et par sokker**
	eht pahr <u>sohk`</u> • kuhr
stockings	**et par strømper**
	eht pahr <u>strurm`</u> • puhr
suit	**en dress** *m* /**drakt** *f*
	ehn drehss/drahkt
sunglasses	**solbriller**
	<u>soo`l</u> • brihl • luhr
sweater	**en genser**
	ehn <u>gehn´</u> • suhr
sweat suit	**en treningsdrakt**
	ehn <u>treh`</u> • nihngs • drahkt
swimming trunks	**en badebukse**
	ehn <u>bah`</u> • duh • buk • suh

swimsuit	**en badedrakt**
	ehn bah`•duh•drahkt
T-shirt	**en T-skjorte**
	ehn teh´•shu•rtuh
tie	**et slips**
	eht shlips
undershirt	**en trøye**
	ehn trury•uh

FABRIC

I'd like…	**Jeg vil gjerne ha…**
	yay vihl yar`•nuh hah…
cotton	**bomull**
	bum`•mewl
denim	**denim**
	deh´•nihm
lace	**knipling**
	knihp`•lihng
leather	**lær**
	lar
linen	**lin**
	leen
silk	**silke**
	sihl`•kuh
wool	**ull**
	ewl
Is it machine washable?	**Kan den vaskes i maskin?**
	kahn dehn vahs`•kuhs ih mah•shee´n

SHOES

I'd like…	**Jeg vil gjerne ha…**
	yay vihl yar`•nuh hah…

boots	**støvler**	
	sturv` • luhr	
flat shoes	**lavhælte sko**	
	lahv` • hehl • tuh skoo	
high heels	**sko med høye hæler**	
	skoo meh hury` • uh heh `luhrl	
loafers	**mokkasiner**	
	muk • kah • see´ • nuhr	
sandals	**sandaler**	
	sahn • dah´ • luhr	
shoes	**sko**	
	skoo	
slippers	**tøfler**	
	turf´ • luhr	
sneakers	**turnsko**	
	tewrn´ • skoo	
In size…	**I størrelse…**	
	ih sturr` • rehl • suh…	

For Numbers, see page 22.

SIZES

small (S)	**liten**	
	lee` • tuhn	
medium (M)	**mellomstor**	
	mehl` • ohm • stoor	
large (L)	**stor**	
	stoor	
extra large (XL)	**ekstra stor**	
	ehks´ • trah stoor	
petite	**liten (klesstørrelse)**	
	leet • ehn kleh • sturr • ehls • eh	
plus size	**ekstra stor**	
	ehk • strah stur	

NEWSAGENT & TOBACCONIST

Do you sell English-language books/newspapers?	**Har dere bøker/aviser på engelsk?** h*ah*r deh` • ruh *bur´* • kuhr/ ah • *vee´* • suhr poh *ehng´* • ehlsk
I'd like…	**Jeg vil gjerne ha…** yay vihl *yar`* • nuh h*ah*…
candy [sweets]	**noen godter** *noo`* • uhn *goht`* • tuhr
chewing gum	**en pakke tyggegummi** ehn *pahk`* • kuh *tuig`* • guh • gew • mi
a chocolate bar	**en sjokoladeplate** ehn shu • ku • *lah´* • duh • pl*ah* • tuh
cigars	**noen sigarer** *noo`* • uhn sih • *gah´* • ruhr
a pack/carton of cigarettes	**en pakke/kartong sigaretter** ehn *pahk`* • kuh/kahr • *tohng´* sih • gah • *reht´* • tuhr
a lighter	**en lighter** ehn *lie´* • tuhr
a magazine	**et blad** eht bl*ah*
matches	**fyrstikker** *fuir`* • stihk • kuhr
a newspaper	**en avis** ehn ah • *vee´*s
a road/town map of…	**et veikart/bykart over…** eht *vay`* • kahrt/*bui´* • kahrt aw • *vuhr*…
stamps	**noen frimerker** *noo`* • uhn *free´* • mehr • kuhr

PHOTOGRAPHY

I'd like...camera.	**Jeg vil gjerne ha...** *yay vihl <u>yar</u>` • nuh hah...*
an automatic	**et helautomatisk kamera** *eht <u>hehl</u>` • ev • tu • mah • tihsk <u>kah</u>´ • meh • rah*
a digital	**et digitalkamera** *eht dih • gih • <u>tah</u>´l • kah • meh • rah*
a disposable	**et engangskamera** *eht <u>ehn</u>´ • gangs • kah • meh • rah*
I'd like...	**Jeg vil gjerne ha...** *yay vihl <u>yar</u>` • nuh • hah...*
a battery	**et batteri** *eht baht • tuh • ree´*
digital prints	**papirkopi av digitale bilder** *pah • <u>pee</u>´r • ku • pee ah dih • gih • <u>tah</u>´ • luh <u>bihl</u>` • duhr*
a memory card	**en minnebrikke** *ehn <u>mihn</u>´ • nuh • brihk • kuh*
Can I print digital photos here?	**Lager dere papirkopier av digitale bilder?** *<u>lah</u>` • guhr <u>deh</u>` • ruh pah • <u>pee</u>´r • ku • pih • uhr ah dih • gih • <u>tah</u>´ • luh <u>bihl</u>` • duhr*

SOUVENIRS

(rose-painted) bowl	**(rosemalt) bolle** _(roo` • suh • mahlt) bohl`_ • luh
candlestick	**lysestake** _lui` • suh • stah • kuh_
cardigan (with Norwegian design)	**lusekofte** _lew` • suh • kohf • tuh_
doll in native costume	**dukke med bunad** _dewk` • kuh meh bew` • nahd_
drinking horn	**drikkehorn** _drihk` • kuh • hoorn_
hunting knife	**jaktkniv** _yahkt´ • kneev_
plate	**asjett** _ah • sheht´_
reindeer skin	**reinsdyrskinn** _reins´ • duir • shihn_
sealskin slippers	**selskinnstøfler** _sehl` • shihns • turf • luhr_
troll	**troll** _trohl_
Viking ship	**vikingskip** _vee` • kihng • sheep_

wooden figurine	**trefigur**
	treh` • fih • gewr
woven runner	**rye**
	rui` • uh
Something typically Norwegian, please.	**Jeg vil gjerne ha noe typisk norsk.**
	yei vihl yar` • nuh hah _noo`_ • uh _tui´_ • pihsk norsk
Can I see this/that?	**Kan jeg få se på denne/den der?**
	kahn yei foh seh poh _dehn`_ • nuh/dehn dar
It's the one in the window/display case.	**Det er den i vinduet/monteren.**
	deh ar dehn ih _vihn`_ • dew • uh/ _mohn´_ • tuhr • uhn
I'd like…	**Jeg vil gjerne ha…**
	yei vihl _yar`_ • nuh hah…
a battery	**et batteri**
	eht baht • tuh • _ree´_
a bracelet	**et armbånd**
	eht _ahrm`_ • bohn
a brooch	**en brosje**
	ehn _broh`_ • shuh
earrings	**et par øreringer**
	eht pahr _ur´_ • ruh • rihng • uhr
a necklace	**et halskjede**
	eht _hahl`s_ • kheh • duh

a ring	**en ring**
	ehn rihng
a watch	**en klokke**
	ehn <u>klohk</u>` • kuh
copper	**kobber**
	<u>kohb</u>` • buhr
crystal	**krystall**
	krui • <u>stahl</u>´
diamond	**diamant**
	dih • ah • <u>mahnt</u>´
white/yellow gold	**hvitt/gult gull**
	*viht/g**ew**lt g**ew**l*
pearl	**perle**
	<u>par</u>` • luh
pewter	**tinn**
	tihn
platinum	**platina**
	<u>plah</u>´ • tih • nah
sterling silver	**sterlingsølv**
	<u>star</u>´ • lihng • surl
Is this real?	**Er den ekte?**
	ar dehn <u>ehk</u>` • tuh
Can you engrave it?	**Kan du få den gravert?**
	*kahn d**ew** foh dehn grah • <u>vehrt</u>´*

Typical souvenirs from Norway include knit items like sweaters and cardigans, gloves and mittens. Other handcrafted pieces like silver, glassware, pottery and hand-painted wooden objects, such as bowls with rose designs, Norwegian trolls, fjord horses and viking ships abound. Art lovers will find that there are also many art galleries across the country. It is a good idea to get local recommendations on where to buy. Goat and reindeer skins as well as furs are also popular.

SPORT & LEISURE

NEED TO KNOW

When's the game?	**Når går kampen?**
	nohr gawr <u>kahm</u>´ • puhn
Where's...?	**Hvor er...?**
	voor ar...
the beach	**stranden**
	<u>strahn</u>´ • nuhn
the park	**parken**
	<u>pahr</u>´ • kuhn
the swimming pool	**svømmebassenget**
	<u>svurm</u>` • muh • bahs • sehng • uh
Is it safe to swim/ dive here?	**Er det trygt å svømme/dykke her?**
	<u>ar</u> deh truikt aw <u>svurm</u>` • muh/ <u>duik</u>` • kuh har
Can I rent [hire] golf clubs?	**Kan jeg leie golfkøller?**
	kahn yay <u>lay</u>` • uh <u>gohlf</u>´ • kurl • luhr
How much per hour?	**Hvor mye koster det per time?**
	voor <u>mui</u>` • uh <u>kohs</u>` • tuhr deh pehr <u>tee</u>´ • muh
How far is it to...?	**Hvor langt er det til...?**
	voor <u>lahngt</u>´ ar deh tihl...
Can you show me on the map?	**Kan du vise meg det på kartet?**
	kahn dew <u>vee</u>` • suh may deh poh <u>kahr</u>´ • tuh

WATCHING SPORT

When's…?	**Når går…?**
	nohr gawr…
the basketball game	**basketballkampen**
	bah´s • kuht • bahl • kahm • puhn
the cycling race	**sykkelløpet**
	suik´ • kuhl • lur • puh
the golf tournament	**golfturneringen**
	gohlf´ • tewr • neh • rihng • uhn
the soccer [football] game	**fotballkampen**
	foot` • bahl • kahm • puhn
the tennis match	**tenniskampen**
	tehn´ • nihs • kahm • puhn
the volleyball game	**volleyballkampen**
	vohl´ • lih • bahl • kahm • puhn
Which teams are playing?	**Hvilke lag spiller?**
	vihl´ • kuh lahg spihl • luhr
Where's the stadium?	**Hvor er stadion?**
	voor ar stah´d • yohn
Where can I place a bet?	**Hvor kan jeg spille på hester?**
	voor kahn yay spihl` • luh poh hehs` • tuhr

Norwegians are very active people and particularly enjoy outdoor sports. Water sports, such as boating, canoeing and fishing are popular, though skiing and hiking are the primary participant sports. In fact, Norwegians boast 4,000 years of skiing, since skis were originally developed as a means of transportation through the snow. Today, there are many ski resorts across Norway and tourist offices can recommend the nearest one for downhill skiing as well as local ski facilities for cross-country skiing. Hiking can be done almost anywhere, but if you're up for an exhilarating experience, try **brevandringer** (guided glacier walks).

PLAYING SPORT

Where's...?	**Hvor er...?**
	voor ar...
the golf course	**golfbanen**
	gohlf´ • bah • nuh
the gym	**trimrommet**
	trihm´ • rum • muh
the park	**parken**
	pahr´ • kuhn
the tennis court	**tennisbanen**
	tehn´ • nihs • bah • nuhn
How much per...?	**Hva koster det per...?**
	vah kohs` • tuhr deh pehr...
day	**dag**
	dahg
hour	**time**
	tee` • muh
game	**spill**
	spihl
round	**runde**
	rewn` • duh
Can I rent [hire]...?	**Kan man leie...?**
	kahn mahn lay` • uh...

golf clubs	**golfkøller**
	gohlf´ • kurl • luhr
equipment	**utstyr**
	_ew`t_ • stuir
a racket	**en racket**
	ehn _rehk´_ • kuht

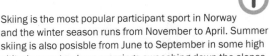

Skiing is the most popular participant sport in Norway and the winter season runs from November to April. Summer skiing is also posisble from June to September in some high altitude resorts where mornings swooshing down the slopes can be combined with afternoon sunbathing. Major ski resorts are located in Geilo, Hafjell, Hemsedal, Lillehammer, Norefjell (the closest to Oslo) and Trysil. Other snow-oriented activities include dog-sledding, ice-fishing, skating, sleigh-riding, snowboarding, snowmobiling and tobogganing.

AT THE BEACH/POOL

Where's the beach/pool?	**Hvor er stranden/svømmebassenget?**
	voor ar _strahn´_ • nuhn/
	svurm` • muh • bah • _sehng_ • uh
Is there...here?	**Fins det...her?**
	fihns deh...har
a kiddie [paddling] pool	**et barnebasseng**
	eht _bahr`_ • _nuh_ • bahs • sehng
an indoor/outdoor pool	**et innendørs/utendørs svømmebasseng**
	eht _ihn`_ • nuhn • durrs/_ew`_ • tuhn • durrs
	svurm` • muh • bahs • sehng
a lifeguard	**badevakt**
	bah` • duh • vahkt
Is it safe...here?	**Er det trygt...her?**
	ar deh truikt...har

to swim	**å svømme**
	oh svurm` • muh
to dive	**å dykke**
	oh duik` • kuh
for children	**for barn**
	fohr bahn
I want to rent [hire]...	**Jeg vil gjerne leie...**
	yay vihl yar` • nuh lay` • uh...
a deck chair	**en fluktstol**
	ehn flewkt´ • stool
diving equipment	**dykkeutstyr**
	duik` • kuh • ewt • stuir
a jet-ski	**en vannscooter**
	ehn vahn` • skew • tuhr
a motorboat	**en motorboat**
	ehn moo´ • toor • bawt
a rowboat	**en robåt**
	ehn roo´ • bawt
snorkling equipment	**snorkleutstyr**
	snohr`k • luh • ewt • stuir
a surfboard	**et surfebrett**
	eht sewr` • fuh • breht
a towel	**et håndkle**
	eht hohng` • kleh
an umbrella	**en parasol**
	ehn pah • rah • sohl´
water-skis	**vannski**
	vahn` • shee
For...hours.	**For...timer.**
	fohr...tee` • muhr

On good summer days the temperatures in Norway can be warm enough to sunbathe and swim. There are possibilities for diving, waterskiing and windsurfing along the coast and on Norway's many lakes. White-water rafting and kayaking are an adrenaline-pumping option on the rivers in Oppland, Hedmark and Sør-Trøndelag.

WINTER SPORTS

Can I have a lift pass for a day/five days?	**Kan jeg få et heiskort for én dag/fem dager?**
	kahn yay faw eht <u>hays</u>`•kort fohr ehn dahg/fehm <u>dah</u>`g•uhr
I'd like to rent [hire]…	**Jeg vil gjerne leie…**
	yay vihl <u>yar</u>`•nuh <u>lay</u>`•uh…
boots	**støvler**
	<u>sturv</u>`•luhr
a helmet	**en hjelm**
	ehn yehlm
poles	**staver**
	<u>stah</u>`•vuhr
skis	**ski**
	shee
a snowboard	**et snøbrett**
	eht <u>snur</u>`•breht
snowshoes	**truger**
	<u>trew</u>`•guhr
These are too big/small.	**Disse er for store/små.**
	<u>dihs</u>`•suh ar fohr <u>stoo</u>´•ruh/smaw
Can I take skiing lessons?	**Kan jeg ta skitimer?**
	kahn yay tah <u>shee</u>´•tee•muhr

I'm a beginner.	**Jeg er nybegynner.**
	yay ar <u>nui</u>` • buh • yuin • nuhr
Can I have a trail [piste] map?	**Kan jeg få et løypekart?**
	kahn yay faw eht <u>lury</u>` • puh • kahrt

OUT IN THE COUNTRY

Can I have a map of…?	**Kan jeg få et kart over…?**
	kahn yay faw eht kart
	<u>aw</u>´ • vuhr…
this region	**dette området**
	<u>deht</u>` • tuh <u>ohm</u>` • raw • duh
the walking routes	**turstier**
	<u>tewr</u>´ • stee • uhr
the bike routes	**sykkelstier**
	<u>suik</u>´ • kuhl • stee • uhr
the trails	**skiløypene**
	<u>shee</u>´ • lury • puh • nuh
Is it an easy/ a difficult trip?	**Er det en lett/vanskelig tur?**
	ar deh ehn leht/<u>vahn</u>´ • skuh • lih tewr
Is it far/steep?	**Er det langt/bratt?**
	ar deh lahngt/braht
How far is it to…?	**Hvor langt er det til…?**
	voor lahngt´ ar deh tihl…
Can you show me on the map?	**Kan du vise meg på kartet?**
	kahn dew <u>vee</u>` • suh may poh kahr´ • tuh
I'm lost.	**Jeg har gått meg bort.**
	yay hahr goht may bu • rt
Where's…?	**Hvor er…?**
	voor ar…
the bridge	**broen**
	<u>broo</u>´ • uhn
the cave	**hulen**
	<u>hew</u>` • luhn

the farm	**gården**
	gawr´ • uhn
the ferry landing	**ferjestedet**
	fer` • yuh • st**eh** • duh
the field	**jordet**
	yoo` • ruh
the fjord	**fjorden**
	f_yoo_´ • ruhn
the forest	**skogen**
	sk_oo_´ • guhn
the glacier	**breen**
	breh´ • uhn
the hill	**bakken**
	bahk` • kuhn
the lake	**innsjøen**
	ihn` • sh**ur** • uhn
the mountain	**fjellet**
	f_yehl_´ • luh
the nature preserve	**nasjonalparken**
	nah • shu • _nah´l_ • par • kuhn
the overlook	**utsikten**
	_ew_`t • sihk • tuhn
the park	**parken**
	pahr´ • kuhn

the path	**stien**
	stee´ • uhn
the peak	**toppen**
	tohp´ • puhn
the picnic area	**turområdet**
	tewr´ • um • raw • duh
the pond	**dammen**
	dahm´ • muhn
the river	**elva**
	ehl´ • vah
the waterfall	**fossen**
	foh´ • suhn

For Asking Directions, see page 64.

Culturally, there is a lot to enjoy in Norway. In summer, many cultural events, including orchestral concerts and operas, are celebrated outdoors. Theater is extremely popular, though most productions are in Norwegian. Classical ballet is performed at the Oslo Opera House and traditional folk dances can be seen across the country.
If you are interested in the visual arts, the Munch museum, named after the internationally-famous Edvard Munch, in Oslo is popular. The extensive National Museum of Art, Architecture and Design is also in Oslo.

TRAVELING WITH CHILDREN

NEED TO KNOW

Is there any discount for children?	**Er det reduksjon for barn?** *ar deh reh • dewk • <u>shoo</u>´n fohr bahrn*
Can you recommend a babysitter?	**Kan du anbefale en barnevakt?** *kahn dew <u>ahn</u>´• buh • fah • luh ehn <u>bahr</u>`• nuh • vahkt*
Could we have a child's seat/ highchair?	**Kan vi få en barnestol/babystol?** *kahn vee faw ehn <u>bahr</u>`• nuh • stool/ <u>beh</u>´• bih • stool*
Where can I change the baby?	**Hvor kan jeg bytte på babyen?** *voor kahn yay <u>buit</u>`• tuh poh <u>beh</u>´• bih • uhn*

OUT & ABOUT

Can you recommend something for the kids?	**Kan du anbefale noe for barna?** *kahn dew <u>ahn</u>´• buh • fah • luh <u>noo</u>`• uh fohr <u>bahr</u>´• nah*
Where's…?	**Hvor er…?** *voor ar…*
the amusement park	**fornøyelsesparken** *fohr • <u>nury</u>´• uhl • suhs • pahr • kuhn*
the arcade	**spillehallen** *spihl • eh • <u>hahl</u> • ehn*
the kiddie [paddling] pool	**plaskebassenget** *<u>plahs</u>`• kuh • bahs • sehng • uh*
the park	**parken** *<u>pahr</u>´• kuhn*

the playground	**lekeplassen**
	leh` • kuh • plahs • suhn
the zoo	**dyrehagen**
	dui` • ruh • hah • guhn
Are kids allowed?	**Er det adgang for barn?**
	ar deh _ahd_` • gahng fohr bahrn
Is it safe for children?	**Er det trygt for barn?**
	ar deh truikt fohr bahrn
Is it suitable for... year olds?	**Passer det for...åringer?**
	pahs` • suhr deh fohr...` • awr • ihng • uhr

For Numbers, see page 22.

BABY ESSENTIALS

Do you have...?	**Har dere...?**
	hahr _deh_` • ruh...
a baby bottle	**en tåteflaske**
	ehn _taw_` • tuh • flahs • kuh
baby wipes	**papirkluter**
	pah • _pee_´r • klew • tuhr
a car seat	**et barnesete**
	eht _bahr_` • nuh • seh • tuh
a children's menu/portion	**en barnemeny/barneporsjon**
	ehn _bahr_` • nuh • meh • nui/ _bahr_` • nuh • poor • shoon
a child's seat/highchair	**en barnestol/babystol**
	ehn _bahr_` • nuh • stool/ _beh_´ • bih • stool
a crib/cot	**en barneseng/sprinkelseng**
	ehn _bahr_` • nuh • sehng/ _sprihng_´ • kul • sehng
diapers [nappies]	**bleier**
	blay` • uhr

formula	**morsmelkerstatning**
	moors´ • mehlk • ehr • staht • nihng
a pacifier [dummy]	**en narresmokk**
	ehn _nahr`_ • ruh • smuk
a playpen	**en lekegrind**
	ehn _leh`_ • kuh • grihn
a stroller	**en gåstol**
[pushchair]	ehn _gaw´_ • stool
Can I breastfeed the baby here?	**Kan jeg amme babyen her?**
	kahn yay _ahm`_ • uh _beh´_ • bih • uhn har
Where can I change the baby?	**Hvor kan jeg bytte på babyen?**
	voor kahn yay _buit´_ • tuh poh
	beh´ • bih • uhn

For Dining with Children, see page 166.

BABYSITTING

Can you recommend a reliable babysitter?	**Kan du anbefale en pålitelig barnevakt?**
	kahn dew _ahn´_ • buh • _fah_ • luh ehn
	poh • _lee´_ • tuh • lih _bahr`_ • nuh • vahkt
What's the charge?	**Hvor mye koster det?**
	voor _mui`_ • uh _kohs`_ • tuhr deh
We'll be back by...	**Vi er tilbake klokken...**
	vee ar tihl • _bah`_ • kuh
	klohk` • kuhn...
I'll be back by...	**Jeg er tilbake til...**
	yay ar tihl • bahk • _eh_ tih
I can be reached at...	**Jeg kan nås på...**
	yay kahn naws poh...
If you need to contact me, call...	**Om du må kontakte meg, ring...**
	awm dew maw kun • takht • _eh_ may _rihng_

HEALTH & SAFETY

EMERGENCIES

NEED TO KNOW

Help!	**Hjelp!**
	yehlp
Go away!	**Gå vekk!**
	gaw vehk
Stop, thief!	**Stopp tyven!**
	stohp tui´ • vuhn
Get a doctor!	**Hent en lege!**
	hehnt ehn leh` • guh
Fire!	**Brann!**
	brahn
I'm lost.	**Jeg har gått meg bort.**
	yay hahr goht may boort
Can you help me?	**Kan du hjelpe meg?**
	kahn dew yehl` • puh may

In an emergency, dial:
112 for the police
110 for the fire brigade
113 for medical emergencies.

POLICE

NEED TO KNOW

Call the police!	**Ring politiet!**
	ring pu•lih•_tee´_•uh
Where's the police station?	**Hvor er politistasjonen?**
	voor ar pu•lih•_tee´_•stah•shoo•nuhn
There's been an accident/attack.	**Det har skjedd en ulykke/et overfall.**
	deh har shehd ehn _ew´_•luik•kuh/ eht _aw`_•vuhr•fahl
My child is missing.	**Barnet mitt er kommet bort.**
	bahr`_•nuh miht ar _kohm`•muht boort
I need...	**Jeg trenger...**
	yay _trehng´_•uhr...
an interpreter	**en tolk**
	ehn tohlk
to contact my lawyer	**å kontakte advokaten min**
	oh kun•_tahk´_•tuh ahd•vu•_kah´_•tuhn mihn
to make a phone call	**å ta en telefon**
	oh tah ehn teh•luh•_foon´_
I'm innocent.	**Jeg er uskyldig.**
	yay ar ew•_shuil´_•dih

CRIME & LOST PROPERTY

I want to report...	**Jeg vil anmelde...**
	yay vihl _ahn´_•meh•luh...
a mugging	**et overfall**
	eht _aw`_•vuhr•fahl
a rape	**en voldtekt**
	ehn _vohl`_•tehkt

a theft	**et tyveri**
	eht tui • vuhr • <u>ee</u>´
I've been robbed/ mugged.	**Jeg har blitt ranet/overfalt.**
	yay hahr bliht <u>rah</u>` • nuht/<u>aw</u>` • vuhr • fahlt
I've lost…	**Jeg har mistet…**
	yay hahr <u>mihs</u>` • tuht…
…has been stolen.	**…er blitt stjålet.**
	…ar bliht <u>styaw</u>` • luht
My backpack	**Ryggsekken min**
	<u>ruig</u>` • sehk • kuhn mihn
My bicycle	**Sykkelen min**
	<u>suik</u>´ • kuhl • uhn mihn
My camera	**Fotoapparatet mitt**
	f<u>oo</u>´ • tu • ahp • pah • raht • uh miht
My (rental) car	**(Leie-)bilen min**
	(<u>lay</u>` • uh) • beel • uhn mihn
My computer	**PCen min**
	<u>peh</u>` • seh • uhn mihn
My credit cards	**Kredittkortet mitt**
	kreh • <u>diht</u>´ • kor • tuh miht
My jewelry	**Smykkene mine**
	<u>smuik</u>` • kuh • nuh <u>mih</u>` • nuh
My money	**Pengene mine**
	<u>pehng</u>` • uh • nuh <u>mih</u>` • nuh

My passport	**Passet mitt**
	pahs´ • suh miht
My purse [handbag]	**Håndvesken min**
	hohn` • vehs • kuhn mihn
My traveler's checks [cheques]	**Reisesjekkene mine**
	ray`_ • suh • shehk • kuh • nuh _mih` • nuh
My wallet	**Lommeboken min**
	lum` • muh • **boo** • kuhn mihn

I need a police report for my insurance claim.	**Jeg trenger en politirapport til forsikringskravet mitt.**
	yay trehng´ • uhr ehn
	pu • lih • **tee´** • rahp • pohrt tihl
	fohr • _sihk´_ • rihngs • krah • vuh miht

Where is the British/ American/Irish embassy?	**Hvor er den britiske/amerikanske/ irske ambassaden?**
	voor ar dehn breet • ihsk • eh/
	ahm • ehr • ee • kahn • skeh/eersk • eh
	ahm • bah • sahd • ehn

I need an interpreter.	**Jeg trenger en tolk.**
	yay trehng • ehr ehn tawlk

HEALTH

FINDING A DOCTOR

Can you recommend a doctor/dentist?	**Kan du anbefale en lege/tannlege?**
	_kahn d**ew** _ahn´_ • buh • f**ah** • luh ehn_
	leh`_ • guh/_tahn` • l**eh** • guh_
Can the doctor come to see me here?	**Kan legen komme hit og undersøke meg?**
	_kahn _leh`_ • guhn _kohm`_ • muh h**ee**t oh_
	ewn` • nuhr • **sur** • kuh may_

NEED TO KNOW

I'm sick [ill].	**Jeg er syk.**
	yay ar suik
I need an English-speaking doctor.	**Jeg trenger en lege som snakker engelsk.**
	yay trehng´•uhr ehn leh`•guh sohm snahk`•kuhr ehng´•ehlsk
It hurts here.	**Det gjør vondt her.**
	deh yurr vunt har
I have a stomachache.	**Jeg har magesmerter.**
	yay hahr mah`•guh•smer•tuhr

I need an English-speaking doctor.	**Jeg trenger en lege som snakker engelsk.**
	yay trehng´•uhr ehn leh`•guh sohm snahk`•kuhr ehng´•ehlsk
What are the office hours?	**Når er det kontortid?**
	nawr ar deh kun•toor´•teed
Can I make an appointment...?	**Kan jeg få time...?**
	kahn yay faw tee`•muh...

for today	**i dag**
	*ih da**h**g*
for tomorrow	**i morgen**
	ih <u>maw</u>` • ruhn
as soon as possible	**så snart som mulig**
	*soh sna**h**rt sohm <u>mew</u>` • lih*
It's urgent.	**Det haster.**
	deh <u>hahs</u>` • tuhr

SYMPTOMS

I'm bleeding.	**Jeg blør.**
	*yay bl**u**rr*
I'm constipated.	**Jeg har forstoppelse.**
	*yay h**a**hr fohr • <u>stohp</u>´ • puhl • suh*
I'm dizzy.	**Jeg er svimmel.**
	yay ar <u>svihm</u>´ • muhl
It hurts here.	**Det gjør vondt her.**
	*deh y**u**rr vunt har*
I have…	**Jeg har…**
	*yay h**a**hr…*
an allergic reaction	**fått en allergisk reaksjon**
	foht ehn ah • <u>ler</u>´ • gihsk reh • ahk • <u>shoo</u>´n
chest pain	**vondt i brystet**
	vunt ih <u>bruis</u>´ • tuh
cramps	**kramper**
	krahm • pehr
diarrhea	**diaré**
	dee • ahr • ehn
an earache	**øreverk**
	<u>ur</u>` • ruh • vehrk
a fever	**feber**
	<u>feh</u>´ • buhr

pain	**smerter**
	smer`•tuhr
a rash	**utslett**
	ew`t•shleht
sprained...	**forstuet...**
	fohr•stew´•uht...
some swelling	**hevelse**
	heh`•vuhl•suh
a stomachache	**magesmerter**
	mah`•guh•smer•tuhr
sunstroke	**fått solstikk**
	foht soo`l•stihk
I've been sick [ill] for...days.	**Jeg har vært syk i...dager.**
	yay hahr vert suik ih... dahg`•uhr
I'm ...months pregnant.	**Jeg er ...måneder gravid.**
	yay ar mawn•ehd•ehr grah•veedk

For Numbers, see page 22.

CONDITIONS

I have...	**Jeg har...**
	yay hahr...
asthma	**astma**
	ahst´•mah
arthritis	**leddgikt**
	lehd`•yihkt
high/low blood pressure	**høyt/lavt blodtrykk**
	huryt/lahvt bloo`•truik
a heart condition	**en hjertesykdom**
	ehn yer`•tuh•suik•dohm
I have epilepsy.	**Jeg har epilepsi.**
	yay hahr eh•phi•lehp•see

I'm allergic to antibiotics/ penicillin.
Jeg er allergisk mot antibiotika/ penicillin.
*yay ar ah • <u>ler´</u> • gihsk moot ahn • tih • bih • <u>**oo**</u>´• tih • kah/ peh • nih • sih • <u>leen´</u>*

I'm on...
Jeg går på...
yay gawr poh...

For Dietary Requirements, see page 164.

YOU MAY HEAR...

Hva er i veien?
vah ar ih <u>vay´</u> • uhn
What's wrong?

Er du allergisk mot noe?
ar dew ah • <u>ler´</u> • gihsk moot <u>noo`</u> • uh
Are you allergic to anything?

Gap opp.
gahp ohp
Open your mouth.

Pust dypt.
pewst duipt
Breathe deeply.

Du bør få foretatt en allmenn undersøkelse.
dew burr foh <u>faw`</u> • ruh • taht ehn <u>ahl`</u> • mehn ewn` • nuhr • sur • kuh • uhl • suh
I want you to go to the hospital.

TREATMENT

Do I need a prescription/ medicine?
Trenger jeg resept/medisin?
trehng • ehr yay rehs • ehpt/meh • dee • seen

Can you prescribe a generic drug [unbranded medication]?
Kan du skrive resept på en generika?
kahn dew skrih • vuh reh • sehpt paw ehn gehn • ehri • kah

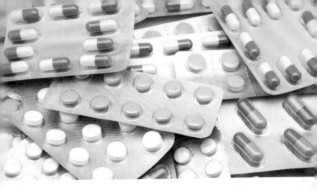

| Where can I get it? | **Hvor får jeg tak i det?** |
| | *voor fawr yay tahk ee deh* |

HOSPITAL

Please notify my family.	**Vær snill å underrette familien min.**
	var snihl oh <u>ewn`</u> • nuhr • reht • uh fah • <u>mee´</u> lyuhn mihn
I am in pain.	**Jeg har smerter.**
	yay hahr <u>smer`</u> • tuhr
I need a doctor/nurse.	**Jeg trenger en lege/sykepleier.**
	yay trehng´ • uhr ehn <u>leh`</u> • guh/<u>sui`</u> • kuh • play • uhr
What are the visiting hours?	**Når er det besøkstid?**
	nohr ar deh buh • <u>sur´ks</u> • teed
I'm visiting…	**Jeg skal besøke…**
	yay skahl buh • <u>sur´k</u> • uh…

DENTIST

I've broken a tooth.	**Jeg har brukket en tann.**
	yay hahr <u>bruk`</u> • kuht ehn than
I have lost a filling.	**Jeg har mistet en plombe.**
	yay hahr <u>mihs`</u> • tuht ehn <u>plum`</u> • buh

I have a toothache.	**Jeg har tannpine.**
	yay hahr <u>tahn`</u> • pee • nuh
Can you fix my dentures?	**Kan du reparere gebisset?**
	kahn dew reh • pah • <u>reh´</u> • ruh guh • <u>bihs´</u> • suh

For Pharmacy, see page 149.

GYNECOLOGIST

I have menstrual cramps/a vaginal infection.	**Jeg har menstruasjonssmerter/ underlivsbetennelse.**
	yay hahr mehn • strew • ah • <u>shoo´</u> ns • smer • tuhr/ ewn` • nuhr • leevs • buh • tehn • nuhl • suh
I missed my period.	**Jeg har ikke hatt menstruasjon.**
	yay hahr <u>ihk`</u> • kuh haht mehn • strew • ah • <u>shoo´n</u>
I'm on the Pill.	**Jeg tar p-piller.**
	yay tahr <u>peh´</u> • pil • luhr
I'm (not) pregnant.	**Jeg er (ikke) gravid.**
	yay ar (<u>ihk`</u> • kuh) grah • <u>vee´d</u>
I haven't had a period for… months.	**Jeg har ikke hatt menstruasjon på… måneder.**
	yay hahr <u>ihk`</u> • kuh haht mehn • strew • ah • <u>shoo´n</u> poh… <u>maw`</u> • nuhd • uhr

For Numbers, see page 22.

OPTICIAN

I've lost…	**Jeg har mistet…**
	yay hahr <u>mihs`</u> • tuht…

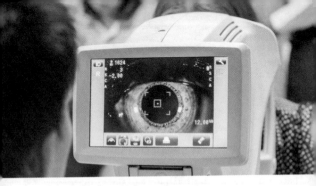

a contact lens	**en kontaktlinse**
	ehn kun • <u>tahkt</u>´ • lihn • suh
my glasses	**brillene mine**
	<u>brihl</u>` • luh • nuh <u>mih</u>` • nuh
a lens	**et brilleglass**
	eht <u>brihl</u>` • luh • glahs

PAYMENT & INSURANCE

How much?	**Hvor mye koster det?**
	voor <u>mui</u>` • uh <u>kohs</u>` • tuhr deh
Can I pay by credit card?	**Kan jeg betale med kredittkort?**
	kahn yay buh • <u>tah</u>´ • luh meh kreh • <u>diht</u>´ • kort
I have insurance.	**Jeg har forsikring.**
	yay hahr fohr • <u>sihk</u>´ • rihng
Can I have a receipt for my health insurance?	**Kan jeg få en kvittering for sykeforsikringen?**
	kahn yay faw ehn kviht • <u>teh</u>´ • rihng fohr <u>sui</u>`k • uh • fohr • sihk • rihng • uhn

For Money, see page 32.

PHARMACY

NEED TO KNOW

Where's the nearest pharmacy [chemist's]?	**Hvor er nærmeste apotek?** *voor ar ner̲ • mehs • tuh ah • pu • teh ́k*
What time does the pharmacy [chemist's] open/close?	**Når åpner/stenger apoteket?** *nohr aw̲ ̀p • nuhr/ stehng̲ ̀ • uhr ah • pu • teh ́k • uh*
What would you recommend for...?	**Hva anbefaler du mot...?** *vah ahn̲ ́ • buh • fah • luhr dew moot...*
How much should I take?	**Hvor mye skal jeg ta?** *voor mui̲ ̀ • uh skahl yay tah*
Can you fill [make up] this prescription for me?	**Kan du gjøre i stand denne resepten for meg?** *kahn dew yur̲ ̀ • ruh ih stahn dehn̲ ́ • nuh reh • sehp ́ • tuhn fohr may*
I'm allergic to...	**Jeg er allergisk mot...** *yay ar ah • ler̲ ́ • gihsk moot...*

WHAT TO TAKE

How much should I take?	**Hvor mye skal jeg ta?** *voor mui̲ ̀ • uh skahl yay tah*
How often?	**Hvor ofte?** *voor ohf̲ ̀ • tuh*
I'm taking...	**Jeg tar...** *yay tahr...*
Are there side effects?	**Er det noen bivirkninger?** *ar̲ deh noo̲ ̀ • uhn bee ́ • vihrk • nihng • uhr*

Is it safe for children?	**Er det trygt for barn?** *ar deht • eh trygt fawr bahn*

In Norway, the **apotek** (pharmacy) fills medical prescriptions, while the **parfymeri** (drug store) sells non-prescription items, such as toiletries and cosmetics. Most pharmacies are open during regular business hours: 9:00 a.m. to 6:00 p.m. on weekdays. Certain pharmacies may also be open on weekends and a few are open 24 hours a day.

YOU MAY SEE...

EN GANG/TRE GANGER OM DAGEN	once/three times a day
DRÅPE	drop
TABLETT	tablet
TESKJE	teaspoon
...MÅLTIDER	...meals
ETTER	after
FØR	before
MED	with
PÅ TOM MAGE	on an empty stomach
Å SVELGE HEL	swallow whole
KAN FORÅRSAKE TRETTHET	may cause drowsiness
IKKE INNTA ORALT	do not ingest
KUN TIL UTVORTES BRUK	for external use only

HEALTH PROBLEMS

I'd like something for...	**Jeg vil gjerne ha noe mot...** *yay vihl yar̀ • nuh hah noò • uh moot...*

a cold	**forkjølelse**
	fohr • <u>khur´</u> • luhl • suh
a cough	**hoste**
	<u>hus`</u> • tuh
diarrhea	**diarré**
	dih • ah • <u>reh´</u>
insect bites	**insektstikk**
	<u>ihn`</u> • sehkt • stihk
motion [travel]	**reisesyke**
sickness	*<u>ray`</u> • suh • **sui** • kuh*
a sore throat	**sår hals**
	*s**a**wr hahls*
sunburn	**solforbrenning**
	<u>soo`l</u> • fohr • brehn • nihng
an upset stomach	**urolig mage**
	*ew • <u>roo´</u> • lih **mah`** • guh*

BASIC SUPPLIES

I'd like...	**Jeg vil gjerne ha...**
	*yay vihl <u>yar`</u> • nuh h**ah**...*
acetaminophen	**paracetamol**
[paracetamol]	*pah • rah • seht • tahm • <u>oo´l</u>*

antiseptic cream	**en antiseptisk salve**
	ehn ahn • tih • sehp´ • tihsk sahl` • vuh
aspirin	**aspirin**
	ahs • pih • ree´n
a bandage	**plaster**
[plaster]	*plahs´ • tuhr*
a comb	**en kam**
	ehn kahm
condoms	**kondomer**
	kun • doo´ • muhr
contact lens	**kontaktlinsevæske**
solution	*kun • tahkt´ • lihn • suh • vehs • kuh*
deodorant	**en deodorant**
	ehn deh • u • du rahnt´
a hairbrush	**en hårbørste**
	ehn haw`r • burr • stuh
hair spray	**hårlakk**
	hawr` • lahk
ibuprofen	**ibuprofen**
	ih • bew • pru • fehn´
insect repellent	**et insektmiddel**
	eht ihn` • sehkt • mihd • duhl
a nail file	**en neglefil**
	ehn nayl` • uh • feel

a razor/disposable razor	**en barberhøvel/engangshøvel**
	ehn bahr•__behr´__•hurv•vuhl/ ehn´•gahngs•hurv•vuhl
razor blades	**barberblader**
	bahr•__behr´__•blah•uhr
sanitary napkins	**sanitetsbind**
	sah•nih•__teh´ts__•bihn
shampoo/ conditioner	**en sjampo/hårbalsam**
	ehn __shahm´__•pu/__haw`r__•bahl•sahm
soap	**en såpe**
	ehn saw`•puh
sunscreen	**solkrem**
	__soo`l__•krehm
tampons	**tamponger**
	tahm•pohng´•uhr
tissues	**papirlommetørklær**
	pah•__pee´r__•lum•muh•turrk•luhr
toilet paper	**toalettpapir**
	tu•ah•__leht´__•pah•peer
a toothbrush	**en tannbørste**
	ehn __tahn`__•burr•stuh
toothpaste	**en tannpasta**
	ehn __tahn`__•pahst•ah

For Baby Essentials, see page 134.

CHILD HEALTH & EMERGENCY

Can you recommend a pediatrician?	**Kan du anbefale en barnelege?**
	kahn dew __ahn´__•buh•fah•luh ehn __bahr`__•nuh•leh•guh
My child is allergic to…	**Barnet mitt er allergisk mot…**
	__bahr´__•nuh miht ar ah•__lehr´__•gihsk moot…

My child is missing.	**Barnet mitt er kommet bort.**
	bahr´ • nuh miht ar <u>kohm</u>` • muht boort
Have you seen a boy/girl?	**Har du sett en gutt/jente?**
	hahr dew seht ehn gewt/<u>yehn</u>` • tuh

For Police, see page 139.

DISABLED TRAVELERS

NEED TO KNOW

Is there...?	**Er det...?**
	ar deh...
access for the disabled	**adkomst for bevegelseshemmede**
	<u>ahd</u>` • kohmst fohr buh • <u>veh</u>´ • guhl • suhs • hem • muhd • uh
a wheelchair ramp	**en rullestolsrampe**
	ehn <u>rewl</u>` • luh • stools • rahm • puh
a handicapped-[disabled-]accessible toilet	**et handikaptoalett**
	eht <u>hehn</u>´ • dih • kehp • tu • ah • leht
I need...	**Jeg trenger...**
	yay <u>trehng</u>´ • uhr...
assistance	**hjelp**
	yehlp
an elevator [lift]	**en heis**
	ehn hays
a ground-floor room	**et rom i første etasje**
	eht rum ih <u>furr</u>` • stuh eh • <u>tah</u>´ • shuh

ASKING FOR ASSISTANCE

I'm disabled.	**Jeg er bevegelseshemmet.**
	yay ar buh • <u>veh</u>´ • guhl • suhs • hem • muht
I'm visually/hearing impaired.	**Jeg er synshemmet/hørselshemmet.**
	yay ar <u>sui</u>´ns • hehm • muht/
	<u>hurr</u>´ • sehls • hehm • muht
I'm unable to walk far.	**Jeg kan ikke gå langt.**
	yay kahn <u>ihk</u>` • kuh gaw lahngt
I'm unable to use the stairs.	**Jeg kan ikke bruke trappen.**
	yay kahn <u>ihk</u>` • kuh <u>brew</u>` • kuh
	<u>trahp</u>´ • puhn
Can I bring my wheelchair?	**Kan jeg komme i rullestol?**
	kahn yay <u>kohm</u>` • muh ih <u>rewl</u>` • luh • stool
Are guide dogs permitted?	**Er det adgang for førerhunder?**
	ar deh <u>ahd</u>` • gahng fohr
	<u>fur</u>` • ruhr • hewn • nuhr
Can you help me?	**Kan du hjelpe meg?**
	kahn dew <u>yehl</u>` • puh may
Can you open/hold the door?	**Kan du åpne/holde døra?**
	kahn dew <u>awp</u>` • nuh/<u>hohl</u>` • luh <u>dur</u>´ • rah

For Emergencies, see page 138.

FOOD & DRINK

EATING OUT

NEED TO KNOW

Can you recommend a good restaurant/ bar?	**Kan du anbefale en bra restaurant/bar?** *kahn dew <u>ahn´</u> • buh • fah • luh ehn brah rehs • tew • <u>rahng´</u>/bahr*
Is there a traditional Norwegian/an inexpensive restaurant near here?	**Fins det en typisk norsk/billig restaurant i nærheten?** *fihns deh ehn <u>tui´</u> • pihsk nohrsk/ <u>bihl`</u> • lih rehs • tew • <u>rahng´</u> ih <u>nar´</u> • heh • tuhn*
A table for…	**Et bord til…** *eht boor tihl…*
Could we have a table here/ there?	**Kan vi få et bord her/der?** *kahn vee faw eht eht boor har/dar*
Could we have a table in the corner?	**Kan vi få et hjørnebord?** *kahn vee faw eht eht <u>yur`n</u> • uh • boor*
I'm waiting for someone.	**Jeg venter på noen.** *yay <u>vehn`</u> • tuhr poh <u>noo`</u> • uhn*
Where is the restroom [toilet]?	**Hvor er toalettet?** *voor ar tu • ah • <u>leht´</u> • tuh*
Can I have a menu?	**Kan jeg få se menyen?** *kahn yay faw seh meh • <u>nui´</u> • uhn*
What do you recommend?	**Hva kan du anbefale?** *vah kahn dew <u>ahn´</u> • buh • fah • luh*
I'd like…	**Jeg vil gjerne ha…** *yay vihl <u>ya`</u>r • nuh hah…*
Can I have more…?	**Kan jeg få litt mer…?** *kahn yay faw liht mehr…*

Enjoy your meal!	**God appetitt!**
	gu ahp • puh • tiht´
Can I have the check [bill]?	**Kan jeg få regningen?**
	kahn yay faw ray` • nihng • uhn
Is service included?	**Er service inkludert?**
	ar surr´ • vihs ing • klew • dehrt´
Can I pay by credit card?	**Kan jeg betale med kredittkort?**
	kahn yay buh • tah´ • luh meh kreh • diht´ • kohrt
Can I have a receipt?	**Kan jeg få kvittering?**
	kahn yay faw kviht • teh´ • rihng
Thank you.	**Takk.**
	tahk

WHERE TO EAT

Can you recommend…?	**Kan du anbefale…?**
	kahn dew ahn´ • buh • fah • luh…
a restaurant	**en restaurant**
	ehn rehs • tew • rahng´
a bar	**en bar**
	ehn bahr
a cafe	**en kafé**
	ehn kah • feh´
an authentic/ a non-touristy restaurant	**en autentisk/turistfri restaurant**
	ehn ev • tehn • tihsk/tew • rihst • free rehs • tew • rahng
a cheap restaurant	**en billig restaurant**
	ehn bihl • ih rehs • tew • rahng
an expensive restaurant	**en dyr restaurant**
	ehn dyr rehs • tew • rahng

a fast-food place	**en hurtigmatrestaurant**
	ehn hewr`•tih•maht•rehs•tew•rahng
a restaurant	**en restaurant med god utsikt**
with a good view	*ehn rehs•tew•rahng meh gu ewt•sihkt*

RESERVATIONS & PREFERENCES

I'd like to reserve	**Jeg vil gjerne bestille et bord…**
a table…	*yay vihl ya`r•nuh buhs•tihl´•luh eht boor…*
for four	**til fire**
	tihl fee`•ruh
for this evening	**til i kveld**
	tihl ih kvehl
for tomorrow at…	**til i morgen klokken…**
	tihl ih maw`•ruhn klohk`•kuhn…
A table for two,	**Et bord til to, takk.**
please.	*eht boor´ tihl too tahk*
We have	**Vi har bestilt bord.**
a reservation.	*vee hahr buhs•tihlt´ boor*
My name is…	**Jeg heter…**
	yay heh`•tuhr…
Could we have…?	**Kan vi få et…?**
	kahn vee faw…
a table here/there	**et bord her/der**
	eht boor har/dar
a table in the	**et hjørnebord**
corner	*eht yur`•nuh•boor*
a table by the	**vindusbord**
window	*vihn`•dews•boor*
Can we sit…	**Kan vi sitte…**
	kahn vee siht•eh
outside	**ute**
	ewte
in the shade	**i skyggen**
	ee shyh•gehn

in the sun	**i solen**
	ee sul • ehn
in a non-smoking area	**i et røykfritt område**
	ee eht ruryk • friht um • raw • deh
Where is the restroom [toilet]?	**Hvor er toalettet?**
	voor ar tu • ah • leht´ • tuh

YOU MAY HEAR...

Har dere bestilt bord?	Do you have a reservation?
hahr deh • ruh buhs • tihlt´ boor	
Hvor mange?	How many?
voor mahn • geh	
Røyk eller røykfritt?	Smoking or non-smoking?
ruryk ehl • ehr ruryk • friht	
Er dere klare til å bestille?	Are you ready to order?
ar deh • ruh klah´ • ruh tihl aw buhs • tihl´ • luh	
Hva skal det være?	What would you like?
vah skahl deh va` • ruh	
Jeg anbefaler...	I recommend...
yay ahn • beh • fahl • ehr	
God appetitt.	Enjoy your meal.
gu ahp • puh • tiht´	

HOW TO ORDER

Waiter/Waitress!	**Servitør!**
	ser • vih • turr´
We're ready to order.	**Vi er klare til å bestille.**
	vee ar klah` • ruh tihl aw buhs • tihl´ • luh
Can I have the wine list?	**Kan jeg få se vinkartet?**
	kahn yay faw seh veen` • kahr • tuh

I'd like…	**Jeg vil gjerne ha…**
	yay vihl ya`r • nuh hah…
a bottle of…	**en flaske…**
	ehn flahs` • kuh…
a carafe of…	**en karaffel…**
	ehn kah • rahf´ • fuhl…
a glass of…	**et glass…**
	eht glahs…
Can I have a menu?	**Kan jeg få se menyen?**
	kahn yay faw seh meh • nui´ • uhn
Do you have…?	**Har dere…?**
	hahr deh` • ruh…
a menu in English	**en meny på engelsk**
	ehn meh • nui´ poh ehng´ • ehlsk
a set menu	**en fast meny**
	ehn fahst meh • nui´
a children's menu	**en barnemeny**
	ehn bahr` • nuh • meh • nui
What do you recommend?	**Hva kan du anbefale?**
	vah kahn dew ahn´ • buh • fah • luh
What's this?	**Hva er dette?**
	vah ar deht` • tuh
What's in it?	**Hva inneholder den/det?**
	vah ihn` • nuh • hawl • luhr dehn/deh
Is it spicy?	**Er den/det sterkt krydret?**
	ar dehn/deh sterkt kruid` • ruht
rare	**råstekt**
	raw` • stehkt
medium	**medium stekt**
	meh´ • dih • ewm stehkt
well-done	**godt stekt**
	goht stehkt
Can I have more…?	**Kan jeg få litt mer…?**
	kahn yay faw liht mehr…

With/Without…	**Med/Uten…**
	meh/ew` • tuhn…
I can't eat…	**Jeg tåler ikke…**
	yay taw´ • luhr ihk` • kuh…
It's to go [take away].	**Jeg tar det med meg.**
	yay tahr´ deh meh may

For Drinks, see page 196.

YOU MAY SEE…

INNGANGSPENGER	cover charge
DAGENS MENY	menu of the day
SPESIALITETER	specials
TIPS (IKKE) INKLUDERT	service (not) included

COOKING METHODS

baked	**bakt**
	bahkt
boiled	**kokt**
	kukt
braised	**braisert**
	brahs • seh´rt
breaded	**panert**
	pah • neh´rt
creamed	**fløtegratinert**
	flur` • tuh • grah • tih • nehrt
diced	**i terninger**
	ih ter` • nihng • uhr
fried	**stekt**
	stehkt

grilled (broiled)	**grillet** _grihl_` • luht
poached	**pochert** pu • _sheh_´rt
roasted	**ovnsstekt** _ohvns_` • stehkt
sautéed	**sautert** soh • _teh_´rt
smoked	**røkt** rurkt
steamed	**dampet** _dahm_` • puht
stewed	**stuet** _stew_` • uht
stuffed	**fylt** fuilt

DIETARY REQUIREMENTS

I'm…	**Jeg er…** yay _ar_…
a diabetic	**diabetiker** dih • ah • _beh_´ • tihk • uhr

lactose intolerant	**laktoseintolerant**
	lahk • __too__ ` • suh • ihn • toh • luh • rahnt
a vegetarian	**vegetarianer**
	veh • guh • tahr • ih • __ah__ ´ • nuhr
vegan	**veganer**
	veh • gah • nehr
I'm allergic to…	**Jeg er allergisk mot…**
	yay ar ah • __lehr__ ´ • gihsk moot…
I can't eat…	**Jeg kan ikke spise…**
	yay kahn __ihk__ ` • kuh __spee__ ` • suh…
dairy	**melkeprodukter**
	__mehl__ ` • kuh • pru • dewk • tuhr
gluten	**gluten**
	__glew__ ´ • tuhn
nuts	**nøtter**
	__nurt__ ´ • tuhr
pork	**svinekjøtt**
	__svee__ ` • nuh • khurt
shellfish	**skalldyr**
	__skahl__ ` • duir
spicy foods	**sterkt krydret mat**
	sterkt __kruid__ ` • ruht maht
wheat	**hvete**
	__veh__ ` • tuh
Is it halal/kosher?	**Er maten halal/kosher?**
	ar __mah__ ´t • uhn hahl • __ahl__ ´/__kohsh__ ´ • uhr
Do you have…?	**Har dere?**
	hahr dehr • eh
skimmed milk	**skummet melk**
	sku • meht mehlk
whole milk	**helmelk**
	hehl • mehlk
soya milk	**soyamelk**
	soy • ah • mehlk

DINING WITH CHILDREN

Do you have children's portions?
Har dere barneporsjoner?
hahr d<u>eh</u>` • ruh
<u>bahr</u>` • nuh • poor • shoon • uhr*

Can I have a highchair/child's seat?
Kan jeg få en babystol/barnestol?
kahn yay faw ehn <u>beh</u>´ • bih • stool/
<u>bahr</u>` • nuh • stool*

Where can I feed/ change the baby?
Hvor kan jeg amme/bytte på babyen?
voor kahn yay <u>ah</u>` • muh/<u>buit</u>` • tuh poh
<u>beh</u>´ • bih • uhn*

Can you warm this?
Kan du varme opp denne?
kahn dew <u>vahr</u>` • muh ohp <u>dehn</u>` • nuh

HOW TO COMPLAIN

How much longer will our food be?
Hvor lenge drøyer det med maten?
vur <u>lehng</u>` • uh <u>drury</u>` • uhr deh meh
<u>maht</u>´ • uhn*

We can't wait any longer.
Vi kan ikke vente lenger.
vee kahn <u>ihk</u>` • kuh <u>vehn</u>` • tuh
<u>lehng</u>` • uhr*

We're leaving.
Vi drar.
vee drahr

That's not what I ordered.	**Dette er ikke det jeg bestilte.** _deht`_ • _tuh ar_ _ihk`_ • _kuh deh yay_ _buh_ • _stihl`_ • _tuh_
I asked for…	**Jeg ba om…** _yay bah um…_
I can't eat this.	**Jeg kan ikke spise dette.** _yay kahn_ _ihk`_ • _kuh_ _spee`_ • _suh deht`_ • _tuh_
This is too…	**Det er for…** _deh ar fohr…_
cold/hot	**kaldt/varmt** _kahlt/varmt_
salty/spicy	**salt/krydret** _sahlt/_ _kruid`_ • _ruht_
tough/bland	**seigt/mildt** _saykt/mihlt_
This isn't clean/ fresh.	**Dette er ikke rent/ferskt.** _deht`_ • _tuh ar_ _ihk`_ • _kuh_ _rehnt/ferskt_

PAYING

Can I have the check [bill]?	**Kan jeg får regningen?** _kahn yay faw_ _rayn`_ • _nihng_ • _uhn_
We'd like to pay separately.	**Vi vil gjerne betale hver for oss.** _vee vihl yar`_ • _nuh buh_ • _tah´_ • _luh var fohr_ _ohs_
It's all together.	**Det er for alt sammen.** _deh ar fohr ahlt_ _sam_ • _muhn_
Is service included?	**Er service inkludert?** _ar_ _surr´_ • _vihs ihng_ • _klew_ • _dehrt´_
What's this amout for?	**Hva står dette beløpet for?** _vah stawr_ _deht`_ • _tuh buh_ • _lur´_ • _puh fohr_
I didn't have that. I had…	**Jeg spiste ikke det. Jeg spiste…** _yay_ _spihs`_ • _tuh_ _ihk`_ • _kuh deh yay_ _spihs`_ • _tuh…_

Can I pay by credit card?	**Kan jeg betale med kredittkort?**
	kahn yay buh • tah´ • luh meh
	kreh • diht´ • kort
Can I have an itemized bill/ a receipt?	**Kan jeg få en spesifisert regning/en kvittering?**
	kahn yay faw ehn speh • sih • fih • seh´rt
	ray` • nihng/ehn kviht • teh´ • rihng
That was a very good meal.	**Maten smakte veldig godt.**
	maht´ • uhn smahk` • tuh vehl` • dih goht
I've already paid.	**Jeg har allerede betalt.**
	yay hahr ahl • eh • rehd • eh beh • tahlt

For Numbers, see page 22.

ⓘ

A 10-15% service charge is typically included in most restaurant bills, though wait staff often receive an extra 5-10% tip.

MEALS & COOKING

> **Frokost** (breakfast) is usually eaten early and
> consists of coffee or tea and **smørbrød** (open-faced
> sandwiches) and perhaps cereal. **Lunsj** (lunch) is typically
> a light meal and may consist of a simple **matpakke** (open-
> faced sandwich brought from home). **Middag** (dinner) is
> often the only hot meal of the day. If **middag** is eaten early,
> then **aftens** (a late night snack), consisting of bread or
> crackers with butter or cheese and cold cuts, is eaten to get
> through the night without going hungry.

BREAKFAST

appelsinjuice	orange juice
ahp • puhl • <u>see</u>´n • yews	
appelsinmarmelade	orange marmalade
ahp • puhl • <u>see</u>´n • mahr • muh • lah • duh	
brød	bread
brur	
bløtkokt/hardkokt egg	soft-boiled/hard-
<u>blur</u>`t • kukt/<u>hah</u>`r • kukt ehg	boiled eggs
egg og bacon/skinke	eggs with bacon/
ehg aw <u>bay</u>´ • kuhn/<u>shihng</u>` • kuh	ham
eggerøre	scrambled eggs
<u>ehg</u>` • guh • rur • ruh	
frokostblanding	cereal
<u>froo</u>´ • kohst • blahn • nihng	
grapefruktjuice	grapefruit juice
<u>grehp</u>´ • frewkt • yews	

havregrøt	oatmeal [porridge]
hahv` • ruh • gr**u**rt	
honning	honey
hohn` • nihng	
juice	fruit juice
yews	
svart/koffeinfri kaffe	black/decaffeinated
svahrt/kohf • fuh • **ee `n** • free kahf´ • fuh	coffee
kaffe med melk/fløte	coffee with milk/
kahf´ • fuh meh mehlk/fl**ur**` • tuh	cream
omelett	omelet
oh • muh • leht´	
ost	cheese
ust	
ristet brød	toast
rihs` • tuht br**ur**	
rundstykke	roll
rewn´ • stuik • kuh	
smør	butter
smurr	
speilegg	fried egg
spayl` • ehg	
syltetøy	jam
suil` • tuh • tury	

te med melk/sitron
teh meh mehlk/siht • roo ´n

tea with milk/lemon

varm sjokolade
vahrm shu • ku • lah` • duh

hot chocolate

varmt vann
varmt vahn

hot water

yoghurt
yoo ´ • gewrt

yogurt

APPETIZERS

blåskjell
blaw` • shehl

mussels

fenalår
feh` • nah • lawr

cured leg of mutton

ferske reker
fehrs` • kuh reh` • kuhr

unshelled shrimp
[prawns]

fiskekabaret
fihs` • kuh • kah • bah • reh

assorted seafood
and vegetables in
aspic

gåselever
gaw` • suh • leh • vuhr

goose liver

gravlaks
grahv` • lahks

cured salmon
flavored with dill

hummer
hum´ • muhr

lobster

kamskjell
kahm` • shehl

scallop

kaviar
kah • vih • ah ´r

caviar

krabbe
krahb` • buh

crab

laks
lahks

salmon

rakørret
rahk` • _urr_ • _ruht_

specially processed, salt-cured and fermented trout

rekecocktail
reh` • _kuh_ • _kohk_ • _tayl_

shrimp [prawn] cocktail

røkelaks
rur` • _kuh_ • _lahks_

smoked salmon

sildebrikke
sihl` • _luh_ • _brihk_ • _kuh_

a variety of herring, served with bread and butter

skinke
shihng` • _kuh_

ham

spekepølse
speh` • _kuh_ • _purl_ • _suh_

smoked, cured sausage

spekeskinke
speh` • _kuh_ • _shihng_ • _kuh_

smoked, cured ham

sursild
sewr´ _sihl_

marinated herring

østers
urs´ • _tehrs_

oysters

SOUP

aspargessuppe
ahs • _pahr´_ • _guhs_ • _sewp_ • _puh_

asparagus soup

betasuppe
beh` • _tah_ • _sewp_ • _puh_

thick meat and vegetable soup

blomkålsuppe
blohm´ • _kawl_ • _sewp_ • _puh_

cauliflower soup

buljong
bewl • _yohng´_

consommé

fiskesuppe
fihs` • _kuh_ • _sewp_ • _puh_

fish soup

fransk løksuppe
frahnsk _lur`k_ • _sewp_ • _puh_

French onion soup

grønnsaksuppe
grurn` • sahk • sewp • puh

vegetable soup

gul ertesuppe
gewl er` • tuh • sewp • puh

yellow pea soup

hummersuppe
hum` • muhr • sewp • puh

lobster soup

kjøttsuppe
khurt` • sewp • puh

meat soup

løksuppe
lur`k • sewp • puh

onion soup

neslesuppe
nehs` • luh • sewp • puh

nettle soup

oksehalesuppe
ohk` • suh • hah • luh • sewp • puh

oxtail soup

sellerisuppe
seh • luh • ree´ • sewp • puh

celery soup

sjampinjongsuppe
shahm • pihn • yohng´ • sewp • puh

button mushroom soup

soppsuppe
sohp` • sewp • puh

field mushroom soup

tomatsuppe
tu • mah´t • sewp • puh

tomato soup

Norwegian cuisine features a wide range of soups, which are often eaten with **flatbrød** (a thin, barley and wheat or barley and rye cracker); this is a common starter. **Fiskesuppe** (fish soup) is very popular along the coast. Other traditional soups involve meat, such as **betasuppe** (meat and vegetable soup), or vegetables, like **gul ertesuppe** (yellow pea soup).

FISH & SEAFOOD

abbor
ahb`•bohr
perch

akkar
ahk`•kahr
squid

ansjos
ahn•shoo´s
anchovies or
marinated sprats

blåskjell
blaw`•shehl
mussels

blekksprut
blehk`•sprewt
octopus

brasme
brahs`•muh
bream

breiflabb
bray`•flahb
angler, also called
frogfish or goosefish

dampet ørret
dahm`•puht urr`•ruht
poached trout

fisk
fihsk
fish

fiskeboller
fihs`•kuh•bohl•luhr
fish balls

fiskekaker
fihs`•kuh•kah•kuhr
fried fish cakes

fiskepudding
fihs`•kuh•pewd•dihng
fish pudding

flyndre
fluin`•druh
flounder

fritert flyndrefilet
friht•eh´rt fluin`•druh•fih•leh
deep fried flounder
fillet

gjedde
yehd`•duh
pike

gravlaks
grah`v•lahks
cured salmon
flavored with dill

hellefisk _hehl`•luh•fihsk_	halibut
hummer _hum´•muhr_	lobster
hvitting _viht`•tihng_	whiting
hyse _hui`•suh_	haddock (western Norway)
kamskjell _kahm`•shel_	scallop
karpe _kahr`•puh_	carp
klippfisk _klihp´•fihsk_	salted and dried fish
kokt torsk _kukt tohrsk_	poached cod
kokt ørret _kukt urr`•ruht_	poached trout
kolje _kohl`•yuh_	haddock (eastern Norway)
krabbe _krahb`•buh_	crab
kreps _krehps_	freshwater crayfish

kveite
kvay` • tuh
halibut

laks
lahks
salmon

lutefisk
lew` • tuh • fihsk
stockfish soaked in lye

lysing
lui` • sihng
hake

makrell
mahk • rehl´
mackerel

piggvar
pihg` • vahr
turbot

plukkfisk
pluk´ • fihsk
stewed codfish

regnbueørret
rayn` • bew • uh • urr • ruht
rainbow trout

reker
reh` • kuhr
shrimp [prawns]

rogn
rohngn
roe

rødspette
rur` • speht • tuh
plaice

sardell
sar • dehl´
canned anchovy

sardin
sar • dee´n
sardine

sei
say
pollock

sik
seek
whitefish

sild
sihl
herring

sjømat
shur` • maht
seafood

sjøørret _shur`•urr•ruht_	sea trout
sjøtunge _shur`•tung•uh_	sole
skalldyr _skahl`•duir_	shellfish
spekesild _speh`•kuh•sihl_	salted herring
steinbit _stayn`•beet_	catfish
stør _sturr_	sturgeon
størje _sturr`•yuh_	tuna
torsk _tohrsk_	cod
tunfisk _tew`n•fihsk_	tuna
tørrfisk _turr´•fihsk_	stockfish
uer _ew`•uhr_	rosefish
ørret _urr`•ruht_	trout

østers _urs´ • tehrs_	oysters
åbor _aw` • bohr_	perch
ål _awl_	eel

MEAT & POULTRY

and _ahn_	duck
bacon _bay´ • kuhn_	bacon
benløse fugler _beh`n • lurs • uh few`l • uhr_	fried, rolled and stuffed slices of veal or beef
biff _bihf_	beef steak
biff med løk _bihf meh lurk_	thick beef steak topped with fried onion
broiler _broi´ • luhr_	chicken
brun lapskaus _brewn lahps´ • kevs_	Norwegian stew in brown gravy
dyrestek _dui` • ruh • stehk_	roast venison
elg _ehlg_	moose
elgbiff _ehlg` • bihf_	moose steak
elgfilet _ehlg` • fih • leh_	moose fillet
elgstek _ehlg` • stehk_	roast moose

fårestek
faw`•ruh•stehk
roast leg of mutton or lamb

fårekjøtt
faw`•ruh•khurt
mutton

fårikål
faw´•rih•kawl
mutton or lamb in cabbage stew

fasan
fah•sah´n
pheasant

gås
gaws
goose

hare
hah`•ruh
hare

hjort
yohrt
deer

høne
hur`•nuh
hen

hvalbiff
vahl`•bihf
whale steak

kalkun
kahl•kew´n
turkey

kalvebrissel
kahl`•vuh•brihs•suhl
calf's sweetbread

kalvekjøtt
kahl`•vuh•khurt
veal

kalvelever
kahl`•vuh•lehv•vuhr
calf's liver

kanin
kah•nee´n
rabbit

karbonade
kahr•bu•nah`•duh
hamburger

kjøttboller
khurt
meatballs

kjøttkaker
khurt`•kahk•uhr
small hamburgers

kjøttpudding
khurt` • pud • dihng
meatloaf

knoke
knoo` • kuh
bone

kotelett
koh • tuh • _leht´_
chop

kylling
khuil` • lihng
chicken

lammekjøtt
lahm • muh • khurt
lamb

lapskaus
lahps´ • kehvs
Norwegian stew with meat, potatoes and root vegetables

lever
lehv´ • vuhr
liver

lys lapskaus
luis _lahps´_ • kehvs
Norwegian stew with diced, salted boiled pork

medisterkaker
meh • _dihs´_ • tuhr • kah • kuhr
small pork and beef hamburgers

medisterpølse
meh • _dihs´_ • tuhr • purl • suh
pork and beef sausage

mørbradstek
mur`r • brahd • stehk
roast sirloin

nyrer
nui` • ruhr
kidneys

oksebryst
ohk` • suh • bruist
beef brisket

oksekjøtt
ohk` • suh • khurt
beef

okserulader
ohk` • suh • rewl • _lah_ • duhr
braised beef rolls

oksestek
ohk` • suh • stehk
roast beef

orrfugl
ohr` • fewl
pinnekjøtt
pihn` • nuh • khurt

pytt i panne
puit • ih • pah` • nuh
pølse
purl` • suh
rådyr
raw´ • duir
rapphøne
rahp` • hur • nuh
reinsdyr
rayns´ • duir
ribbe
rihb` • buh
rype
rui` • puh
skinke
shihng` • kuh
spekeskinke
speh` • kuh • shihng • kuh

black grouse,
a woodland bird
salted and dried
mutton ribs
steamed on twigs
hash or meat and
vegetables
sausage

roe-deer

partridge

reindeer

spareribs

grouse, a mountain
bird
ham

smoked, cured ham

stek	roast (beef, reindeer, moose, etc.)
ste*hk*	
svinekjøtt	pork
_sv**ee**_` • *nuh* • *khurt*	
svor	bacon rind
sv*oor*	[crackling]
sylte	head cheese [brawn]
suil` • *tuh*	
tartarbiff	steak tartare
tahr • _**tah**_´*r* • *bihf*	
T-benstek	T-bone steak
teh´ • *behn* • *stehk*	
vaktel	quail
vahk´ • *tuhl*	
villand	wild duck
vihl` • *lahn*	
wienerschnitzel	breaded veal cutlet
vee´ • *nuhr* • *shniht* • *suhl*	

VEGETABLES & STAPLES

agurk	cucumber
ah • _gewr_´*k*	
anisfrø	aniseed
_**ah**_´ • *nihs* • *frur*	
artisjokker	artichokes
ar • *tih* • _shohk_´ • *kuhr*	
asparges	asparagus
ahs • _pahr_´ • *guhs*	
aubergine	eggplant [aubergine]
aw • *buhr* • _shee_´*n*	
basilikum	basil
bah • _see_´ • *lih* • *kewm*	
blomkål	cauliflower
blohm´ • *kawl*	

bønner _burn`_ • _nuhr_	beans
brokkoli _brohk´_ • _koh_ • _lih_	broccoli
dill _dihl_	dill
erter _ehr´_ • _tuhr_	peas
gresskar _grehs`_ • _kahr_	pumpkin
gressløk _grehs`_ • _lurk_	chives
grønnkål _grurn´_ • _kawl_	kale
gulrøtter _gew`l_ • _rurt_ • _tuhr_	carrots
hodesalat _hoo`_ • _duh_ • _sah_ • _laht_	lettuce
hvitløk _vee´t_ • _lurk_	garlic
ingefær _ihng´_ • _uh_ • _far_	ginger

kål	cabbage
kawl	
kanel	cinnamon
kah • neh´l	
kantareller	chanterelle
kahn • tah • rehl´ • luhr	mushrooms
kapers	capers
kah´ • puhrs	
karri	curry seasoning
kahr´ • rih	
karve	caraway seeds
kahr` • vuh	
kokte poteter	boiled potatoes
kuk` • tuh pu • teh´t • uhr	
komler/komper	potato dumplings
kum` • luhr/kum` • puhr	
linser	lentils
lihn` • suhr	
løk	onions
lurk	
mais	corn
mies	
maiskolbe	corn on the cob
mies´ • kohl • buh	
nellik	clove
nehl´ • lihk	
nepe	turnip
neh` • puh	
nudler	noodles
newd´ • luhr	
nypoteter	new potatoes
nui` • pu • teht • uhr	
paprika	sweet pepper
pahp´ • rih • kah	

persille parsley
pehr•sihl´•luh

pommes frites French fries [chips]
pohm friht

potet potato
pu•teh´t

potetgull potato chips [crisps]
pu•teh´t•gewl

potetkroketter potato croquettes
pu•teh´t•krohk•keht•tuhr

potetmos mashed potatoes
pu•teh´t•moos

potetsalat potato salad
pu•teh´t•sah•laht

purre leeks
pewr`•ruh

raspeball potato dumplings
rahs`•puh•bahl

reddiker radishes
rehd´•dihk•kuhr

ris rice
rees

rosenkål Brussels sprouts
roo´•suhn•kawl

rødbeter beet [beetroot]
rur`•beh•tuhr

rødkål red cabbage
rur´•kawl

salat salad
sah•lah´t

salvie sage
sahl•vee`•uh

selleri celery
sehl•luhr•ee´

sildeball _sihl_` • luh • bahl_	potato dumplings filled with minced salted herring
stekte poteter _stehk_` • tuh pu • teh´t • uhr_	sautéed potatoes
stuede poteter _stew_` • eh • duh pu • teh´t • uhr_	potatoes in a white sauce
sjampinjonger _sham • pihn • yohng´ • uhr_	button mushrooms
sopp _sohp_	mushrooms
spinat _spih • nah´t_	spinach
surkål _sew´r • kawl_	coleslaw
sylteagurk _suil_` • tuh • ah • gewrk_	pickle
timian _tee´ • mih • ahn_	thyme
tomater _tu • maht´ • uhr_	tomatoes

FRUIT

ananas _ahn´ • nah • nahs_	pineapple
appelsin _ahp • puhl • see´n_	orange
aprikos _ahp • rih • koo´s_	apricot
banan _bah • nah´n_	banana
bjørnebær _byur_` • nuh • bar_	blackberries

blåbær
blaw`•bar

blueberries

bringebær
brihng´•uh•bar

raspberries

dadler
dahd´•luhr

dates

druer
drew`•uhr

grapes

einebær
ay`•nuh•bar

juniper berries

eple
ehp`•luh

apple

fersken
fehrs´•kuhn

peach

fikener
fee´•kuhn•uhr

figs

grapefrukt
grehp´•frewkt

grapefruit

hasselnøtter
hahs´•suhl•nurt•tuhr

hazelnuts

jordbær
yoo´r•bar

strawberries

kastanjer
kahs•tahn´•yuhr

chestnuts

kirsebær _khihr´ • suh • bar_	cherries
kokosnøtt _kuk´ • kus • nurt_	coconut
korinter _ku • rihn´ • tuhr_	currants
mandarin _mahn • dah • ree´n_	tangerine
mandler _mahn´d • luhr_	almonds
markjordbær _mahr`k • yoor • bar_	wild strawberries
melon _meh • loo´n_	melon
molter/multer _mohl` • tuhr/mewl` • tuhr_	arctic cloudberries
moreller _mu • rehl´ • luhr_	morello cherries
nektarin _nehk • tah • ree´n_	nectarine
nøtter _nurt´ • tuhr_	nuts
peanøtter _pee´ • ah • nurt • tuhr_	peanuts
plommer _plum` • muhr_	plums
pære _pa` • ruh_	pear
rabarbra _rah • bahr´ • brah_	rhubarb
rips _rihps_	red currants
rognebær _rohng` • nuh • bar_	rowanberries
rosiner _ru • see´ • nuhr_	raisins

sitron _siht • roo´n_	lemon
solbær _soo`l • bar_	black currants
stikkelsbær _stihk´ • kuhls • bar_	gooseberries
svisker _svihs` • kuhr_	prunes
tranebær _trah` • nuh • bar_	cranberries
tyttebær _tuit´ • tuh • bar_	lingonberry
valnøtter _vahl` • nurt • tuhr_	walnuts
vannmelon _vahn` • meh • loon_	watermelon

CHEESE

ekte geitost _ehk` • tuh yayt` • ust_	goat cheese
fløtemysost _flur` • tuh • muis • ust_	mild and sweet, cow's milk cheese
gammelost _gahm` • muhl • ust_	pungent cheese made with skimmed milk
gudbrandsdalsost _gewd` • brahns • dahls • ust_	cow and goat's milk cheese
jarlsbergost _yahrls´ • behrg • ust_	mild, slightly sweet, semi-hard cheese
normannaost _noor • mahn´ • nah • ust_	blue-veined cow's milk cheese
ridderost _rihd´ • duhr • ust_	semi-hard cheese with nutty flavor

DESSERT

bløtkake
blur`t • kah • kuh

layer cake

fruktkompott
frewkt´ • kohm • poht

stewed fruit

hoffdessert
hohf´ • dehs • sar

layers of meringue
and whipped cream,
topped with
chocolate sauce and
toasted almonds

is
ees

ice cream

karamellpudding
kah • rah • mehl´ • pewd • dihng

creme caramel

krem
krehm

whipped cream

mandelkake
mahn´ • duhl • kah • kuh

almond cake

molter/multer med krem
mohl`• tuhr/mewl` tuhr meh krehm

arctic cloudberries
with whipped cream

pære Belle Helene
pa` • ruh behl heh • leh´n

poached pears with
vanilla ice cream and
chocolate

pannekaker — pancakes
pahn`•nuh•kah•kuhr

riskrem — creamed rice
ree´s•krehm

rødgrøt med fløte — berry compote with cream
rur`•grurt meh flur`•tuh

sjokoladepudding — chocolate pudding
shu•ku•lah`•duh•pewd•dihng

sorbett — sorbet
sohr•beht´

sufflé — soufflé
sewf•leh´

terte — fruit cake
tehr`•tuh

tilslørte bondepiker — layers of stewed apples, cookie [biscuit] crumbs, and whipped cream
tihl´•slurr•tuh bun´•nuh•pee•kuhr

vafler med syltetøy — waffles with jam
vahf´•luhr meh suil`•tuh•tury

vaniljesaus — vanilla sauce
vah•nihl`•yuh•sevs

varm eplekake med krem — hot apple pie with whipped cream
vahrm ehp`•luh•kah•kuh meh krehm

SAUCES & CONDIMENTS

ketchup	**ketchup**
	kat•shewp
mustard	**sennep**
	sehn•ehp
pepper	**pepper**
	pehp´•puhr
salt	**salt**
	sahlt

AT THE MARKET

In Norway, there are a few large supermarket chains, such as Rimi, Rema and Kiwi, in addition to many local mini-markets. Keep in mind that most supermarkets and petrol stations do not accept credit cards, a debit card with chip and PIN or cash is the best method of payment.

Where are the carts [trolleys]/baskets?	**Hvor er handlevognene/handlekurvene?** *voor ar <u>hahn`d</u> • <u>luh</u> • vohng • nuh • nuh/ <u>hahn`d</u> • luh • kewr • vuh • nuh*
Where is...?	**Hvor er...?** *voor ar...*
Can I have some of that/those?	**Kan jeg få litt av det/dem?** *kahn yay faw liht a deh/dehm*
Can I taste it?	**Kan jeg smake?** *kahn yay <u>smah`</u> • kuh*
I'd like...	**Jeg vil gjerne ha...** *yay vihl <u>yar`</u> • nuh hah...*
a (half) kilo of...	**en (halv) kilo...** *ehn (hahl) <u>khee´</u> • lu...*

a (half) liter of…	**en (halv) liter…**
	ehn (hahl) lee´ • tuhr…
a piece of…	**et stykke…**
	eht stuik` • kuh…
a slice of…	**en skive…**
	ehn shee` • vuh…
More/Less than that.	**Mer/Mindre enn det.**
	mehr/mihn´ • druh ehn deh
How much?	**Hvor mye koster det?**
	voor mew` • uh kohs` • tuhr deh
Where do I pay?	**Hvor betaler man?**
	voor buh • tah´ • luhr mahn
Can I have a bag?	**Kan jeg få en bærepose?**
	kahn yay faw ehn ba` • ruh • poo • suh
I'm being helped.	**Jeg blir ekspedert.**
	yay bleer ehks • puh • deh´rt

For Money, see page 32.

ⓘ

Measurements in Europe are metric - and that applies
to the weight of food too. If you tend to think in pounds and
ounces, it's worth brushing up on what the metric equivalent
is before you go shopping for fruit and veg in markets
and supermarkets. Five hundred grams, or half a kilo, is
a common quantity to order, and that converts to just over
a pound (17.65 ounces, to be precise).

YOU MAY HEAR...

Kan jeg hjelpe deg?
kahn yay yehl` • puh day

Can I help you?

Hva skal det være?
vah skahl deh va` • ruh

What would you like?

Skal det være noe annet?
skahl deh va` • ruh noo` • uh ahn` • nuht

Anything else?

Det blir...kroner, takk.
deh bleer... kroo`n • uhr tahk

That's...kroner, please.

IN THE KITCHEN

bottle opener	**en flaskeåpner**
	ehn flahs` • kuh • awp • nuhr
bowls	**skåler**
	skaw` • luhr
can opener	**en boksåpner**
	ehn bohks` • awp • nuhr
cheese slicer	**ostehøvel**
	us` • tuh • hur • vuhl
corkscrew	**en korketrekker**
	ehn kohr` • kuh • trehk • kuhr
cups	**kopper**
	kohp` • puhr
forks	**gafler**
	gahf´ • luhr
frying pan	**en stekepanne**
	ehn steh` • kuh • pahn • nuh
glasses	**glass**
	glahs
knives	**kniver**
	kneev` • uhr

measuring cup/ measuring spoon	**et målebeger/en måleskje** _eht maw`•luh•beh•guhr/_ _ehn maw`•luh•sheh_
napkins	**papirservietter** _pah•pee´r•serv•yeht•tuhr_
plates	**tallerkener** _tah•lehr´•kuhn•uhr_
pot	**en gryte** _ehn grui`•tuh_
saucepan	**en kasserolle** _ehn kah•suh•rohl`•luh_
spatula	**en slikkepott** _ehn slihk`•kuh•poht_
spoons	**skjeer** _sheh`•uhrv_

For Domestic Items, see page 80.

DRINKS

NEED TO KNOW

Can I have the wine list/drink menu?	**Kan jeg få se vinkartet/drikkekartet?** *kahn yay faw seh <u>veen</u>` • kahr • tuh/ <u>drihk</u>` • kuh • kahr • tuh*
What do you recommend?	**Hva kan du anbefale?** *vah kahn dew <u>ahn</u>´ • buh • **fah** • luh*
Can I have the house wine?	**Kan jeg få husets vin?** *kahn yay faw <u>hew´s</u> • uhs veen*
Can I buy you a drink?	**Kan jeg by på en drink?** *kahn yay bui poh ehn drihngk*
Cheers!	**Skål!** *sk**aw**l*
A coffee/tea, please.	**En kaffe/te, takk.** *ehn <u>kahf</u>´ • fuh/teh tahk*
Black.	**Svart.** *svahrt*
With...	**Med...** *meh...*
milk	**melk** *mehlk*
sugar	**sukker** *<u>suk</u>´ • kuhr*
artificial sweetener	**søtningsmiddel** *<u>sur</u>`t • nihngs • mihd • duhl*
A glass of..., please.	**Et glass..., takk.** *eht glahs...tahk*
juice	**juice** *y**ew**s*

soda	**soda**
	soo´ • dah
(sparkling/still) water	**vann (med kullsyre/uten kullsyre)**
	vahn (meh kewl` • sui • ruh/ew` • tuhn _kewl` • sui • ruh)_
Is the tap water safe to drink?	**Kan man drikke vann rett fra springen?**
	kahn mahn drihk` • kuh vahn reht frah _sprihng´ • uhn_

NON-ALCOHOLIC DRINKS

ananasjuice
ahn´ • nah • nahs • yews
pineapple juice

appelsinjuice
ahp • puhl • see´n • yews
orange juice

brus
brews
soda

eplesaft
eh` • pluh • sahft
apple juice

grapefruktjuice
grehp´ • frewkt • yews
grapefruit juice

iste
ee`s • teh
iced tea

lettmelk
leht´ • mehlk
low-fat milk

melk
mehlk
milk

mineralvann med kullsyre/
uten kullsyre
mih • nuh • rahl´ • vahn meh kewl` • sui • ruh/
ew` • tuhn kewl` • sui • ruh
sparkling/still mineral water

sitronbrus
siht • roo´n • brews
lemonade

If you're not in the mood for Norwegian beer or spirits, there are a number of other drinks to enjoy. Tea and especially strong coffee are commonly drunk throughout the day. For soft drinks you could try **Solo** (orange-flavored soda) or **Mozell** (apple-flavored soda).

YOU MAY HEAR...

Hva vil du ha å drikke?
vah vihl dew hah aw <u>drihk</u>` • kuh

What would you like to drink?

Med eller uten kullsyre?
*meh <u>ehl</u>´ • luhr <u>ew</u>` • tuhn <u>kewl</u>` • s**ui** • ruh*

Sparkling or still water?

APERITIFS, COCKTAILS & LIQUEURS

akevitt *ah • kuh • <u>viht</u>´*	aquavit
brandy <u>*brehn*</u>´ • dih	brandy
gin tonic *dshihn <u>tohn</u>´ • nihk*	gin and tonic
konjakk *kohn • <u>yahk</u>´*	cognac
likør *lih • <u>kur</u>´r*	liqueur
portvin <u>*poort*</u>´ • veen	port
rom *rum*	rum
sherry <u>*sher*</u>´ • rih	sherry

vermut	vermouth
vehr´ • mewt	
vodka	vodka
vohd´ • kah	
whisky	whisky
vihs´ • kih	

BEER

fatøl	draft [draught] beer
fah `t • url	
flaskeøl	bottled beer
flahs` • kuh • url	
lyst/mørkt øl	light/dark beer
luist/murrkt url	
pils	lager
pihls	
utenlandsk øl	imported beer
ew` • tuhn • lahnsk url	

Beer in Norway is classified by strength. **Lettøl** (beer with low alcohol content) is less than 2.5% alcohol content and **zero** and **vørterøl** are both non-alcoholic. **Pils** (lager) and **bayerøl** (medium-strength dark beer) are relatively low in alcohol content. The strongest beers (6-10%), like **eksportøl** (strong light beer) and **bokkøl** (strong dark beer), are only sold at the **Vinmonopolet** (state-run liquor store). If you are in Norway around Christmas time, be sure to try some of the special limited-edition Christmas brews which are extremely popular with the locals.

Beer, in addition to being drunk on its own, often serves as a chaser to **akevitt** (aquavit), an extremely potent drink distilled from potato and caraway seeds.

WINE

avkjølt	chilled
ah´v • khurlt	
champagne	champagne
shahm • pahn´ • yuh	
fyldig	full-bodied
fuil` • dih	
hvitvin	white
veet´ • veen	
meget tørr	very dry
meh` • guht turr	
musserende	sparkling
mews • seh´ • ruh • nuh	
rødvin	red
rur´ • veen	
rosévin	rosé
roo • seh´ • veen	
søt	sweet
surt	

ON THE MENU

abbor	perch
ahb` • bohr	
agurk	cucumber
ah • gewr´k	
akevitt	aquavit
ah • kuh • viht´	
akkar	squid
ahk` • kahr	
and	duck
ahn	

ananas
ahn´ • nah • nahs

pineapple

ananasjuice
ahn´ • nah • nahs • yews

pineapple juice

anisfrø
ah´ • nihs • frur

aniseed

ansjos
ahn • shoo´s

anchovies or
marinated sprats

appelsin
ahp • puhl • see´n

orange

appelsinjuice
ahp • puhl • see´n • yews

orange juice

appelsinmarmelade
ahp • puhl • see´n • mahr • muh • lah • duh

orange marmalade

aprikos
ahp • rih • koo´s

apricot

artisjokker
ar • tih • shohk´ • kuhr

artichokes

asparges
ahs • pahr´ • guhs

asparagus

aspargessuppe
ahs • pahr´ • guhs • sewp • puh

asparagus soup

aubergine
aw • buhr • shee´n

eggplant [aubergine]

bacon
bay´ • kuhn

bacon

banan
bah • nah´n

banana

basilikum
bah • see´ • lih • kewm

basil

benløse fugler
beh`n • lurs • uh few`l • uhr

fried, rolled and
stuffed slices
of veal or beef

betasuppe
beh` • tah • sewp • puh

thick meat and
vegetable soup

biff
bihf

beef steak

bjørnebær
byur`r • nuh • bar

blackberries

blomkål
blohm´ • kawl

cauliflower

blomkålsuppe
blohm´ • kawl • sewp • puh

cauliflower soup

bløtkake
blur`t • kah • kuh

layer cake

blåbær
blaw` • bar

blueberries

blåskjell
blaw` • shehl

mussels

blekksprut
blehk` • sprewt

octopus

brandy
brehn´ • dih

brandy

brasme
brahs` • muh

bream

brekkbønner
brehk´ • burn • nuhr

French beans

bringebær
brihng´ • uh • bar

raspberries

broiler _broi´_ • luhr	chicken
brokkoli _brohk´_ • koh • lih	broccoli
brisling _brihs`_ • lihng	sprat, brisling
brun lapskaus brewn _lahps´_ • kevs	Norwegian stew in brown gravy
brus brews	soda
brød brur	bread
buljong bewl • _yohng´_	consommé
bønner _burn`_ • nuhr	beans
dadler _dahd´_ • luhr	dates
dill dihl	dill
druer _drew`_ • uhr	grapes
dyrestek _dui`_ • ruh • stehk	roast venison

egg
ehg

eggs

eggerøre
ehg` • guh • rur • ruh

scrambled eggs

einebær
ay` • nuh • bar

juniper berries

ekte geitost
ehk` • tuh yayt` • ust

goat cheese

elg
ehlg

moose

elgbiff
ehlg` • bihf

moose steak

elgfilet
ehlg` • fih • leh

fillet of moose

elgstek
ehlg` • stehk

roast moose

eple
ehp` • luh

apple

eplekake
ehp` • luh • kah • kuh

apple pie

eplesaft
eh` • pluh • sahft

apple juice

erter
ehr´ • tuhr

peas

fasan
fah • sah´n

pheasant

fatøl
fah`t • url

draft [draught] beer

fenalår
feh` • nah • lawr

cured leg of mutton

fersken
fehrs´ • kuhn

peach

fikener
fee` • kuhn • uhr

figs

fisk
fihsk
fish

fiskeboller
<u>fihs`</u> • kuh • bohl • luhr
fish balls

fiskekabaret
<u>fihs`</u> • kuh • kah • bah • reh
assorted seafood and vegetables in aspic

fiskepudding
<u>fihs`</u> • kuh • pewd • dihng
fish pudding

fiskesuppe
<u>fihs`</u> • kuh • sewp • puh
fish soup

flyndre
<u>fluin`</u> • druh
flounder

fløtemysost
fl<u>ur`</u> • tuh • m<u>uis</u> • ust
mild and sweet cow's milk cheese

fransk løksuppe
frahnsk <u>lur`k</u> • sewp • puh
French onion soup

frokostblanding
<u>froo´</u> • kohst • blahn • nihng
cereal

fruktkompott
<u>frewkt´</u> • kohm • poht
stewed fruit

fårekjøtt
<u>faw`</u> • ruh • khurt
mutton

fårestek
<u>faw`</u> • ruh • st<u>eh</u>k
roast leg of mutton or lamb

fårikål
<u>faw´</u> • rih • kawl
mutton or lamb in cabbage stew

gammelost
<u>gahm`</u> • muhl • ust
pungent cheese made with skimmed milk

gin tonic
dshihn <u>tohn´</u> • nihk
gin and tonic

gjedde
<u>yehd`</u> • duh
pike

grapefrukt
<u>grehp´</u> • frewkt
grapefruit

grapefruktjuice
grehp´ • frewkt • yews

grapefruit juice

gravlaks
grah `v • lahks

cured salmon flavored with dill

gresskar
grehs` • kahr

pumpkin

gressløk
grehs` • lurk

chives

grønnkål
grurn´ • kawl

kale

grønnsaksuppe
grurn` • sahk • sewp • puh

vegetable soup

gudbrandsdalsost
gewd` • brahns • dahls • ust

cow and goat's milk cheese

gul ertesuppe
gewl er´ • tuh • sewp • puh

yellow pea soup

gulrøtter
gew`l • rurt • tuhr

carrots

gås
gaws

goose

gåselever
gaw` • suh • leh • vuhr

goose liver

hare
hah` • ruh

hare

harestek
hah` • ruh • stehk
roast hare

hasselnøtter
hahs´ • suhl • nurt • tuhr
hazelnuts

havregrøt
hahv` • ruh • grurt
porridge

hellefisk
hehl` • luh • fihsk
halibut

hjort
yohrt
deer

hjortesadel
yohr` • tuh • sah • duhl
saddle of deer

hodesalat
hoo • duh • sah • laht
lettuce

hoffdessert
hohf´ • dehs • sar
layers of meringue and whipped cream, topped with chocolate sauce and toasted almonds

honning
hohn` • nihng
honey

hummer
hum´ • muhr
lobster

hvalbiff
vahl` • bihf
whale steak

hvitløk garlic
vee´t • lurk

hvitting whiting
viht` • tihng

hvitvin white wine
veet´ • veen

hyse haddock (western
hui` • suh Norway)

høne hen
hur` • nuh

ingefær ginger
ihng´ • uh • far

is ice cream
ees

iste iced tea
ee`s • teh

jarlsbergost mild, slightly sweet,
yahrls´ • behrg • ust semi-hard cheese

jordbær strawberries
yoor´ • bar

juice fruit juice
yews

kaffe coffee
kahf´ • fuh

kalkun turkey
kahl • kew´n

kalvebrissel calf's sweetbread
kahl` • vuh • brihs • suhl

kalvekjøtt veal
kahl` • vuh • khurt

kalvemedaljonger small round fillet of
kahl` • vuh • meh • dahl • yohng • uhr veal

kalvelever calf's liver
kahl` • vuh • lehv • vuhr

kamskjell scallop
kahm` • shel

kanel _kah • neh´l_	cinnamon
kanin _kah • nee´n_	rabbit
kapers _kah´ • puhrs_	capers
karbonade _kahr • bu • nah` • duh_	hamburger
karpe _kahr` • puh_	carp
kastanjer _kahs • tahn´ • yuhr_	chestnuts
karri _kahr´ • rih_	curry seasoning
karve _kahr` • vuh_	caraway seeds
kaviar _kah • vih • ah´r_	caviar
kirsebær _khihr´ • suh • bar_	cherries
kjøttboller _khurt` • bohl • uhr_	meatballs
kjøttkaker _khurt` • kahk • uhr_	small hamburgers
kjøttpudding _khurt` • pud • dihng_	meatloaf
kjøttsuppe _khurt` • sewp • puh_	meat soup
klippfisk _klihp´ • fihsk_	salted and dried cod
knoke _knoo` • kuh_	bone
kokosnøtt _kuk´ • kus • nurt_	coconut

kolje _kohl_` • _yuh_	haddock (eastern Norway)
korinter _ku_ • _rihn´_ • _tuhr_	currants
kotelett _koh_ • _tuh_ • _leht´_	chop
krabbe _krahb_` • _buh_	crab
kreps _krehps_	freshwater crayfish
kveite _kvay_` • _tuh_	halibut
kylling _khuil_` • _lihng_	chicken
kål _kawl_	cabbage
kålrabi/kålrot _kawl_ • _rah´_ • _bih/kawl_` • _root_	rutabaga [swede BE]
kantareller _kahn_ • _tah_ • _rehl´_ • _luhr_	chanterelle mushrooms
karamellpudding _kah_ • _rah_ • _mehl´_ • _pewd_ • _dihng_	creme caramel
kokte poteter _kuk_` • _tuh pu_ • _teh´t_ • _uhr_	boiled potatoes

komler/komper _kum`_ • _luhr/kum`_ • _puhr_	potato dumplings (western Norway)
konjakk _kohn_ • _yahk´_	cognac
krem _krehm_	whipped cream
laks _lahks_	salmon
lammebog _lahm`_ • _muh_ • _boog_	shoulder of lamb
lammebryst _lahm`_ • _muh_ • _bruist_	brisket of lamb
lammekjøtt _lahm`_ • _muh_ • _khurt_	lamb
lammelår _lahm`_ • _muh_ • _lawr_	leg of lamb
lammesadel _lahm`_ • _muh_ • _sah_ • _duhl_	saddle of lamb
lammestek _lahm`_ • _muh_ • _stehk_	roast lamb
lapskaus _lahps´_ • _kevs_	Norwegian stew with meat, potatoes and vegetables

lettmelk
leht` • mehlk
low-fat milk

lever
lehv´ • vuhr
liver

likør
lih • _kur´r_
liqueur

linser
lihn` • suhr
lentils

lungemos
lung` • uh • **moos**
ground [minced] lungs and onions

lutefisk
lew` • tuh • fihsk
stockfish soaked in lye

lys lapskaus
luis lahps´ • kevs
Norwegian stew with diced, salted and boiled pork

løk
lurk
onions

løksuppe
lur`k • sewp • puh
onion soup

mais
mies
corn

maiskolbe
mies´ • kohl • buh
corn on the cob

mandarin
mahn • dah • _ree´n_
tangerine

mandelkake
mahn´ • duhl • **kah** • kuh
almond cake

mandler
mahn´d • luhr
almonds

makrell
mahk • _rehl´_
mackerel

markjordbær
mahr`k • yoor • bar
wild strawberries

medisterkaker
meh • _dihs´_ • tuhr • **kah** • kuhr
small pork and beef hamburgers

medisterpølse
meh • dihs´ • tuhr • purl • suh
pork and beef sausage

melk
mehlk
milk

melon
meh • loo´n
melon

milkshake
mihlk´ • shayk
milkshake

mineralvann
mih • nuh • rahl´ • vahn
mineral water

molter/multer
mohl` • tuhr/mewl´ • tuhr
arctic cloudberries

moreller
mu • rehl´ • luhr
morello cherries

mørbradstek
mur´r • brahd • stehk
roast sirloin

nektarin
nehk • tah • ree´n
nectarine

nellik
nehl´ • lihk
clove

neslesuppe
nehs` • luh • sewp • puh
nettle soup

nepe
neh` • puh
turnip

normannaost
noor • mahn´ • nah • ust
blue-veined cow's milk cheese

nudler
newd´ • luhr
noodles

nypoteter
nui` • pu • teht • uhr
new potatoes

nyrer
nui` • ruhr
kidneys

nøtter
nurt´ • tuhr
nuts

oksebryst
<u>ohk</u>` • suh • bruist

brisket of beef

oksefilet
<u>ohk</u>` • suh • fih • l**e**h

fillet of beef

oksehalesuppe
<u>ohk</u>` • suh • hah • luh • sewp • puh

oxtail soup

oksekam
<u>ohk</u>` • suh • kahm

loin

oksekjøtt
<u>ohk</u>` • suh • khurt

beef

okserulader
<u>ohk</u>` • suh • rewl • **lah** • duhr

braised beef rolls

oksestek
<u>ohk</u>` • suh • st**e**hk

roast beef

omelett
oh • muh • <u>leht</u>´

omelet

orrfugl
<u>ohr</u>` • fewl

black grouse,
a woodland bird

ost
ust

cheese

pannekaker
<u>pahn</u>` • nuh • **kah** • kuhr

pancakes

paprika
<u>pahp</u>´ • rih • kah

sweet pepper

peanøtter
pee´ • ah • nurt • tuhr

peanuts

pepper
pehp´ • puhr

pepper

persille
pehr • sihl` • luh

parsley

piggvar
pihg` • vahr

turbot

pils
pihls

lager

pinnekjøtt
pihn` • nuh • khurt

salted and dried
mutton ribs steamed
on twigs

plommer
plum` • muhr

plums

pommes frites
pohm friht

French fries [chips]

portvin
poort´ • veen

port wine

potet
pu • teh´t

potato

potetgull
pu • teh´t • gewl

potato chips [crisps]

potetkroketter
pu • teh´t • krohk • keht • tuhr

potato croquettes

potetmos
pu • teh´t • moos

mashed potatoes

potetsalat
pu • teh´t • sah • laht

potato salad

purre
pewr` • ruh

leeks

pølse
purl` • suh

sausage

pære
pa` • ruh

pear

pære Belle Helene
_pa`_ • _ruh behl heh •_ _leh ´n_

poached pears with vanilla ice cream and chocolate

rabarbra
rah • _bahr´_ • _brah_

rhubarb

rakørret
rah`k • _urr • ruht_

salt-cured and fermented trout

raspeball
rahs` • _puh • bahl_

potato dumplings

reddiker
rehd´ • _dihk • kuhr_

radishes

regnbueørret
rayn` • _bew • uh • urr • ruht_

rainbow trout

rekecocktail
reh` • _kuh • kohk • tayl_

shrimp [prawn] cocktail

reker
reh` • _kuhr_

shrimp [prawns]

rips
rihps

red currants

ris
rees

rice

ristet brød
rihs` • _tuht brur_

toast

rogn
rohngn

roe

rognebær
rohng` • _nuh • bar_

rowanberries

rosenkål
roo´ • _suhn • kawl_

Brussels sprouts

rosiner
_ru •_ _see´_ • _nuhr_

raisins

rundstykke
rewn´ • _stuik • kuh_

roll

rødbeter
rur` • _beh • tuhr_

beet [beetroot]

rødkål
rur´ • kawl

red cabbage

rødspette
rur` • speht • tuh

plaice

røkelaks
rur` • kuh • lahks

smoked salmon

røye
rury` • uh

char

rådyr
raw´ • duir

roe-deer

rådyrsadel
raw´ • duir • sah • duhl

saddle of venison

rådyrstek
raw´ • duir • stehk

roast venison

ragu
rah • gew´

ragout

rapphøne
rahp` • hur • nuh

partridge

reinsdyr
rayns´ • duir

reindeer

reinsdyrmedaljonger
rayns´ • duir • meh • dahl • yohng • uhr

small, round fillets of reindeer

reinsdyrstek
rayns´ • duir • stehk

roast reindeer

ribbe
rihb`•buh — spareribs

ridderost
rihd´•duhr•ust — semi-hard cheese with nutty flavor

riskrem
ree´s•krehm — creamed rice with red berry sauce

roastbiff
rohst´•bihf — broiled steak

rom
rum — rum

rosévin
roo•seh´•veen — rosé wine

rype
rui`•puh — grouse, a mountain bird

rødgrøt med fløte
rur`•grurt meh flur`•tuh — berry compote with cream

rødvin
rur´•veen — red wine

salat
sah•lah´t — salad

salt
sahlt — salt

saltkjøttlapskaus
sahlt`•khurt•lahps´•kevs — Norwegian stew with diced, salted and boiled pork

salvie
sahl•vee`•uh — sage

sardell
sar•dehl´ — canned anchovy

sardin
sar•dee´n — sardine

sei
say — pollock

selleri
sehl•luhr•ee´ — celery

sellerisuppe
seh • luh • <u>ree´</u> • sewp • puh

celery soup

sherry
<u>sher´</u> • rih

sherry

sik
seek

whitefish

sild
sihl

herring

sildeball
<u>sihl`</u> • luh • bahl

potato dumplings filled with minced salted herring

sitron
siht • <u>roo´</u> n

lemon

sitronbrus
siht • <u>roo´</u> n • brews

lemonade

sjampinjonger
sham • pihn • <u>yohng´</u> • uhr

button mushrooms

sjampinjongsuppe
shahm • pihn • <u>yohng´</u> • sewp • puh

button mushroom soup

sjokoladepudding
shu • ku • <u>lah`</u> • duh • pewd • dihng

chocolate pudding

sjømat
<u>shur`</u> • maht

seafood

sjøørret
<u>shur`</u> • urr • ruht

sea trout

sjøtunge
<u>shur`</u> • tung • uh

sole

skalldyr
<u>skahl`</u> • duir

shellfish

skinke
<u>shihng`</u> • kuh

ham

slettvar
<u>sleht`</u> • vahr

brill

smør
smurr

butter

solbær
soo´l • bar

black currants

sopp
sohp

mushrooms

sorbett
sohr • beht´

sorbet

spinat
spih • nah´t

spinach

steinbit
stayn` • beet

catfish

stek
stehk

roast

stekte poteter
stehk` • tuh pu • teh´t • uhr

sautéed potatoes

stikkelsbær
stihk´ • kuhls • bar

gooseberries

stuede poteter
stew` • eh • duh pu • teh´t • uhr

potatoes in a white sauce

stør
sturr

sturgeon

størje
sturr` • yuh

tuna

sufflé
sewf • leh´

soufflé

surkål
sew´r • kawl

coleslaw

sursild
sew´r • sihl

marinated herring

svinefilet
svee` • nuh • fih • leh

fillet of pork

svinekam
svee` • nuh • kahm

loin of pork

svinekjøtt
svee` • nuh • khurt

pork

svinestek
svee` • nuh • stehk

roast pork

svisker _svihs`_ • _kuhr_	prunes
svor _svoor_	bacon rind [crackling]
sylte _suil`_ • _tuh_	head cheese [brawn]
sylteagurk _suil`_ • _tuh_ • _ah_ • _gewrk_	pickled gherkin
syltetøy _suil`_ • _tuh_ • _tury_	jam
tartarbiff _tahr_ • _**tah´r**_ • _bihf_	steak tartare
T-benstek _teh´_ • _behn_ • _stehk_	T-bone steak
te _teh_	tea
terte _tehr`_ • _tuh_	fruit cake
tilslørte bondepiker _tihl´_ • _slurr_ • _tuh_ _bun´_ • _nuh_ • _pee_ • _kuhr_	layers of stewed apples, cookie [biscuit] crumbs and whipped cream
timian _tee´_ • _mih_ • _ahn_	thyme

tomater	tomatoes
tu • maht´ • uhr	
tomatsuppe	tomato soup
tu • mah´t • sewp • puh	
torsk	cod
tohrsk	
tranebær	cranberries
trah` • nuh • bar	
tunfisk	tuna
tew`n • fihsk	
tunge	tongue
tung` • uh	
tyttebær	lingonberry
tuit´ • tuh • bar	
tørrfisk	stockfish
turr´ • fihsk	
uer	rosefish (seafood)
ew` • uhr	
vafler	waffles
vahf´ • luhr	
vaktel	quail
vahk´ • tuhl	
valnøtter	walnuts
vahl´ • nurt • tuhr	
vaniljesaus	vanilla sauce
vah • nihl` • yuh • sevs	
vannmelon	watermelon
vahn` • meh • loon	
varm sjokolade	hot chocolate
vahrm shu • ku • lah` • duh	
vermut	vermouth
vehr´ • mewt	
villand	wild duck
vihl` • lahn	

vin *veen*	wine
vodka <u>vohd´</u>•kah	vodka
whisky <u>vihs´</u>•kih	whisky
wienerschnitzel <u>vee´</u>•nuhr•shniht•suhl	breaded veal cutlet
yoghurt <u>yoo´</u>•gewrt	yogurt
øl url	beer
ørret <u>urr`</u>•ruht	trout
østers <u>urs´</u>•tehrs	oysters
åbor <u>aw`</u>•bohr	perch
ål awl	eel

GOING OUT

GOING OUT

NEED TO KNOW

What is there to do at night?	**Hva kan man gjøre om kvelden?** *vah kahn mahn yur` • ruh ohm kvehl´ • uhn*
Do you have a program of events?	**Har du en oversikt over ting som skjer?** *hahr dew ehn aw` • vuhr • sihkt aw´ • vuhr tihng sohm shehr*
What's playing at the movies [cinema] tonight?	**Hvilke filmer vises på kino i kveld?** *vihl` • kuh fihl` • muhr vee` • suhs poh khee´ • nu ih kvehl*
Where's...?	**Hvor er...?** *voor ar...*
the downtown area	**sentrum** *sehn´ • trewm*
the bar	**baren** *bahr´ • uhn*
the dance club	**diskoteket** *dihs • ku • teh´ • kuh*
What's the admission charge?	**Hva koster det å komme inn?** *vah kohs` • tuhr deh oh kohm` • muh ihn*

ENTERTAINMENT

Can you recommend…?	**Kan du anbefale…?**
	kahn dew <u>ahn´</u> • buh • fah • luh…
a concert	**en konsert**
	ehn kohn • <u>sehrt´</u>
a movie	**en film**
	ehn fihlm
an opera	**en opera**
	ehn <u>oo´</u> • puh • rah
a play	**et teaterstykke**
	*eht teh • <u>**ah´**</u> • tuhr • stuik • kuh*
When does it start/end?	**Når begynner/slutter det?**
	norh buh • <u>yuin´</u> • nuhr/<u>slew`</u> • tuhr deh
What's the dress code?	**Hvordan bør man være kledt?**
	<u>voor´</u> • dahn burr mahn <u>va`</u> • ruh kleht
I like…	**Jeg liker…**
	yay <u>lee´</u> • kuhr…
classical music	**klassisk musikk**
	<u>klahs´</u> • sihsk mew • <u>sihk´</u>
folk music	**folkemusikk**
	<u>fohl`</u> • kuh • mew • sihk
jazz	**jazz**
	yahs
pop music	**pop**
	pohp
rap	**rap**
	rehp

For Tickets, see page 45.

YOU MAY HEAR...

Vennligst skru av alle mobiltelefoner.
Turn off your cell
[mobile] phones.
vehn´ • lihkst skr**ew** ah <u>ahl</u>` • luh
mu • <u>**bee**´l</u> • tehl • uh • **foo** • nuhr

NIGHTLIFE

What is there to do at night?	**Hva kan man gjøre om kvelden?**
	vah kahn mahn <u>yur</u>` • ruh um <u>kvehl</u>´ • uhn
Can you recommend...?	**Kan du anbefale...?**
	kahn dew <u>ahn</u>´ • buh • **fah** • luh...
a cabaret	**en kabaret**
	ehn kahb • ahr • eh
a club with	**en nattklubb med ... Musikk**
Music	_ehn naht • klewb meh mews • ihk_
a dance club	**et diskotek**
	eht dihs • ku • **teh**´k
a gay club	**en homseklubb**
	ehn <u>hum</u>` • suh • klewb
a nightclub	**en nattklubb**
	<u>naht</u>` • klewb

Is there live music?	**Er det levende musikk der?**
	ar deh leh`•vuhn•uh mew•sihk´ dar
How do I get there?	**Hvordan kommer jeg dit?**
	voor´•dahn kohm´•muhr yay deet
What's the admission charge?	**Hva koster det å komme inn?**
	vah kohs`•tuhr deh oh kohm`•muh ihn
Let's go dancing.	**La oss gå ut og danse.**
	lah ohs gaw ewt oh dahn`•suh
Is this area safe at night?	**Er dette området trygt om natten?**
	ar deht•eh awm•rawd•eht trygt awm naht•ehn

For The Dating Game, see page 230.

The capital offers endless options for going out in pubs, bars, cafes and nightclubs. Many clubs offer live music and attract DJs and musicians from around the world. Oslo also has a growing jazz scene.

All restaurants, bars and nightclubs are smoke-free indoors, though many set up outdoor tables in summer and protection for smokers in the winter. Keep in mind that alcohol is considerably more expensive in Norway than in other countries and many clubs enforce age restrictions.

ROMANCE

NEED TO KNOW

Would you like to go out for a drink/meal?	**Skal vi gå og ta en drink/ut og spise?** *skahl vee gaw oh tah ehn dringk/ewt oh spee`•suh*
What are your plans for tonight/tomorrow?	**Hva gjør du i kveld/i morgen?** *vah yurr dew ih kvehl/ih maw`•ruhn*
Can I have your number?	**Kan jeg få nummeret ditt?** *kahn yay faw num´•muhr•uh diht*
Can I join you?	**Er det opptatt her?** *ar deh awp•that har*
Can I buy you a drink?	**Kan jeg by på en drink?** *kahn yay bui poh ehn drihngk*
I like you.	**Jeg liker deg.** *yay lee´•kuhr day*
I love you.	**Jeg elsker deg.** *yay ehls`•kuhr day*

THE DATING GAME

Would you like to go out for coffee?	**Skal vi gå og ta en kaffe?** *skahl vee gaw oh tah ehn kahf´•fuh*
Would you like to go out for a drink/for dinner?	**Har du lyst å ta en drink/gå og spise middag?** *hahr dew lyst aw tah ehn drihnk/gaw awg spih•seh mihd•ahg*

What are your plans for...?	**Hva gjør du...?**
	vah yurr dew...
tonight	**i kveld**
	ih kvehl
tomorrow	**i morgen**
	ih maw` • ruhn
this weekend	**i helgen**
	ih hehl´ • guhn
Where would you like to go?	**Hvor vil du dra?**
	voor vihl dew drah
I'd like to go to...	**Jeg vil gjerne dra til...**
	yay vihl ya`r • nuh drah tihl...
Do you like...?	**Liker du...?**
	lee´ • kuhr dew...
Can I have your number/e-mail?	**Kan jeg få nummeret ditt/ e-postadressen din?**
	kahn yay faw num´ • muh • ruh diht/ eh´ • pohst • ahd • rehs • suhn dihn
Are you on Facebook/ Twitter?	**Er du på Facebook/Twitter?**
	Ar dew paw feis • bewk/tviht • ehr
Can I join you?	**Kan jeg slå meg ned her?**
	kahn yay slaw may nehd har

You're very attractive.	**Du er svært tiltrekkende.** *dew ar svart <u>tihl</u>´• trehk • kuhn • uh*
Should we go somewhere quieter?	**Skal vi gå til et roligere sted?** *skahl vee gaw tihl eht <u>roo</u>`• lih • uh • ruh stehd*

For Communications, see page 84.

ACCEPTING & REJECTING

I'd love to, thanks.	**Takk, det vil jeg gjerne.** *tahk deh vihl yay <u>ya</u>`r • nuh*
Where should we meet?	**Hvor skal vi møtes?** *voor skahl vee <u>mur</u>`• tuhs*
Let's meet at the bar/your hotel.	**Vi møtes i baren/på hotellet ditt.** *vee <u>mur</u>`• tuhs ee bah´• ruhn/poh hu • <u>tehl</u>´• luh diht*
I'll come by at…	**Jeg henter deg…** *yay <u>hehn</u>`• tuhr day…*
What's your address?	**Hva er adressen din?** *vah ar ahd • <u>rehs</u>´• suhn dihn*
Thanks, but I'm busy.	**Takk, men jeg er dessverre opptatt.** *tahk mehn yay ar dehs • <u>vehr</u>´• ruh ohp´• taht*
I'm not interested.	**Jeg er ikke interessert.** *yay ar <u>ihk</u>`• kuh ihn • truhs • seh´rt*
Leave me alone.	**Vær så snill å la meg være i fred.** *var soh snihl oh lah may <u>va</u>`• ruh ih freh*
Stop bothering me!	**Slutt å plage meg!** *slewt oh <u>plah</u>`• guh may*

For Time, see page 45.

GETTING INTIMATE

Can I hug/kiss you?	**Kan jeg holde rundt/kysse deg?**
	kahn yay hohl` • luh rewnt/khuis` • suh day
Yes.	**Ja.**
	yah
No.	**Nei.**
	nay
Stop!	**Stopp!**
	stohp
I love you.	**Jeg elsker deg.**
	yay ehls` • kuhr day

SEXUAL PREFERENCES

Are you gay?	**Er du homofil?**
	ar dew hu • mu • fee´l
I'm…	**Jeg er…**
	yay ar…
heterosexual	**heterofil**
	heh • teh • ru • fee´l
homosexual	**homofil**
	hu • mu • fee´l
bisexual	**bifil**
	bih • fee´l
Do you like men/ women?	**Liker du menn/kvinner?**
	lee´ • kuhr dew mehn/kvihn` • nuhr

DICTIONARY

ENGLISH–NORWEGIAN

A

a (common nouns) en;
(neuter nouns) et
access (internet)
v bruke (internett)
accessories tilbehør
accident ulykke
accommodation
innkvartering
account konto
acetaminophen
paracetamol
acupuncture akupunktur
adapter adapter
address adresse
admission adgang
after etter
afternoon ettermiddag
air conditioning
klimaanlegg
airline flyselskap
airmail luftpost
airport flyplass
aisle midtgang
aisle seat sete ved
midtgangen
all alt

allergic allergisk
allergic reaction allergisk
reaksjon
allowed tillatt
alter v endre
alternate route annen rute
aluminum
foil aluminiumsfolie
amazing praktfull
ambulance sykebil
American adj amerikansk;
n amerikaner
amusement
park fornøyelsespark
anemic blodfattig
antibiotic antibiotikum
antique antikvitet
antiques store
antikvitetshandel
antiseptic cream
antiseptisk salve
any noe
anyone noen
anything noe
apartment leilighet
appetizer forrett
appointment avtale

adj adjective	**BE** British English	**prep** preposition
adv adverb	**n** noun	**v** verb

arcade spillehall
area område
area code
  retningsnummer
aromatherapy
  aromaterapi
around (nearby) rundt
arrival ankomst
arrive v komme frem
arthritis leddgikt
ask v spørre
aspirin aspirin
asthma astma
at ved
ATM minibank
attack overfall
attractive tiltrekkende
automatic adj automatisk

B

baby baby
baby bottle tåteflaske
baby wipes papirkluter
babysitter barnevakt
back adv
  (direction) tilbake;
  n (body part) rygg
backpack ryggsekk
bag (carrier) bærepose
baggage [BE] bagasje
baggage claim
  bagasjemottak
bakery bakeri
bandage bandasje

bank (finance) bank
bar (place) bar
barber herrefrisør
basket (store) handlekurv
basketball basketball
bathroom bad
battery batteri
battleground slagsted
be v være
beach strand
beautiful vakker
bed seng
before før
beginner begynner
behind bak
beige beige
belt belte
best best
bicycle sykkel
big stor
bike route sykkelsti
bikini bikini
bill regning
birthday fødselsdag
black svart
bland smakløs
blanket ullteppe
bleed v blø
blind blind
blood blod
blood pressure blodtrykk
blouse bluse
blue blå
boat båt

boarding ombordstigning
boarding pass
  ombordstigningskort
book bok
bookstore bokhandel
boot støvel
boring kjedelig
botanical gardens
  botanisk hage
bother v plage
bottle flaske
bottle opener flaskeåpner
bowl (container) bolle
boy gutt
boyfriend kjæreste
bra behå
bracelet armbånd
break down v (car) få
  motorstopp
breakfast frokost
breathe v puste
bridge bro
briefs underbukse
bring v (something) ta med
British britisk
broken (bone) brukket;
  (out of order) gått i
  stykker
brooch brosje
broom feiekost
brown brun
bug (insect) insekt
bus buss

bus station busstasjon
bus stop bussholdeplass
business forretning
business card visittkort
business center
  forretningssenter
busy opptatt
but men
buy v kjøpe; **(treat)** by på

C

cable car n taubane
cafe kafé
call n (phone) samtale;
  v (phone) ringe
camera kamera
camp v campe
campsite n campingplass
can v (be able to) kunne;
  n (container) boks
can opener boksåpner
cancel v annullere
candlestick lysestake
car bil
car hire [BE] bilutleie
car park [BE]
  parkeringsplass
car rental bilutleie
car seat barnesete
carafe karaffel
card kort
cardigan
  (Norwegian) lusekofte

carry v bære
carry-on (luggage)
  håndbagasje
cart (shopping)
  handlevogn;
  (luggage) tralle
carton kartong
cash v løse inn; n kontanter
cashier kasse
castle slott
cathedral domkirke
cave hule
cell phone mobil
certificate of authenticity
  ekthetssertifikat
chair stol
chair lift stolheis
change v (alter) endre;
  (baby)
  bytte på;
  (transport) bytte;
  v (money) veksle;
  n (money) vekslepenger
cheap billig
check (payment) sjekk;
  (restaurant) regning
check in v (airport) sjekke
  inn
check-in desk
  innsjekkingsskranke
check out v sjekke ut
cheers skål
cheese slicer ostehøvel

chemical toilet kjemisk
  toalett
chemist [BE] apotek
cheque [BE] sjekk
chest bryst
chest pain vondt i brystet
chewing gum tyggegummi
child barn
children's menu
  barnemeny
children's portion
  barneporsjon
church kirke
cigar sigar
cigarette sigarett
cinema [BE] kino
city by
classical music klassisk
  musikk
clean adj ren; v vaske
cleaning supplies
  rengjøringsmidler
clear v (ATM) slette
cliff klippe
cling film [BE] plastfolie
close v stenge
closed stengt
clothing store klesbutikk
coat (man's) frakk;
  (woman's) kåpe
coin mynt
cold adj kald;
  n (illness) forkjølelse

colleague kollega
color farge
comb kam
come v komme
computer datamaskin
concert konsert
conditioner (hair)
 hårbalsam
condom kondom
conference konferanse
confirm v bekrefte
constipation forstoppelse
contact lens kontaktlinse
contact lens solution
 kontaktlinsevæske
convention hall
 konferansesenter
contain v inneholde
control n kontroll
cooking facilities
 kokemuligheter
copper kobber
corkscrew korketrekker
corner hjørne
cost v koste
cot [BE] (child's)
 sprinkelseng
cotton bomull
cough hoste
country land
country code landkode
countryside land
cover charge
 inngangspenger

cream (ointment) salve
credit card kredittkort
crib (child's) barneseng
crystal krystall
cup kopp
currency valuta
currency exchange office
 vekslingskontor
customs toll
cut v (with scissors)
 klippe
cute søt
cycling sykling
cycling race sykkelløp

D

dairy melkeprodukter
damage v skade
dance v danse
dance club diskotek
dark mørk
day dag
deaf døv
deck chair fluktstol
declare v (customs)
 fortolle
deep dyp
delay forsinkelse
delayed forsinket
delete v (computer) slette
delicatessen
 delikatesseforretning
denim dongeri
dentist tannlege

denture gebiss
deodorant deodorant
department store
 stormagasin
departure avgang
deposit (down payment)
 depositum
detergent vaskemiddel
diabetic diabetiker
diamond diamant
diaper bleie
diarrhea diarré
dictionary ordbok
diesel diesel
difficult vanskelig
digital digital
digital camera
 digitalkamera
digital photo digitalt bilde
digital print papirkopi av et
 digitalt bilde
dinner middag
direction retning
dirty skitten
disabled
 bevegelseshemmet
discount rabatt
dish n (plate) fat; (food)
 rett
dish detergent
 oppvaskmiddel
dishwasher
 oppvaskmaskin
display case monter

disposable camera
 engangskamera
disposable razor
 engangshøvel
dive v dykke
diving equipment
 dykkeutstyr
divorced skilt
dizzy svimmel
do v gjøre
doctor lege
dog hund
doll dukke
dollar dollar
domestic innenlands
door dør
double dobbel
double bed dobbeltseng
double room dobbeltrom
down ned
downtown sentrum
drag lift skitrekk
dress kjole
dress code kleskode
drink v drikke; n drikk
drink menu drikkekart
drive v kjøre
driver's license førerkort
driving licence
 [BE] førerkort
drop (liquid) dråpe
drowsiness søvnighet
dry tørr
dry cleaner renseri

dummy [BE] (baby's)
narresmokk
duty (customs) toll
duty-free tollfri

E

earache øreverk
earring ørering
east øst
easy lett
eat v spise
economy class
turistklasse
electrical outlet strømuttak
elevator heis
e-mail n (message)
e-post; v sende e-post
e-mail address
e-postadresse
emergency exit nødutgang
empty adj tom; v tømme
end n slutt; v slutte
English engelsk
English-speaking
engelsktalende
engrave v gravere
enjoy v nyte
enter v gå inn
equipment utstyr
escalator rulletrapp
e-ticket e-billett
excess luggage overvektig
bagasje

evening kveld
event begivenhet
exchange v veksle
exchange rate
vekslingskurs
excursion utflukt
excuse v unnskylde
exit n utgang
expensive dyr
express ekspress
express mail ekspresspost
extension (phone) linje
extra ekstra
extra large ekstra stor
eye øye
eyebrow øyenbryn

F

face ansikt
facial ansiktsbehandling
family familie
fan (appliance) vifte
far langt
farm bondegård
fast hurtig
fax n faks; v fakse
fax number faksnummer
fee gebyr
feed v mate
ferry ferge
ferry landing fergested
fever feber
field jorde

fill (a prescription) v gjøre
  i stand
fill out v fylle ut
fill up v fylle
filling (tooth) plombe
fine (OK) bra
fire (open) ild;
  (disaster) brann
fire door branndør
first class første klasse
fit v passe
fitting room prøverom
fix v reparere
fjord fjord
flight flyavgang
floor etasje
flower blomst
folk music folkemusikk
food mat
foot fot
football [BE] fotball
football game
  [BE] fotballkamp
for for
forest skog
fork gaffel
form (document) skjema
formula
  morsmelkerstatning
fountain fontene
free fri
freezer fryser
fresh fersk

friend venn
from fra
frying pan stekepanne
full full
full time heltid

G

game (match) kamp
garbage bag søppelsekk
garden hage
gas (car) bensin
gas station bensinstasjon
gate utgang
get v (find) få tak i
get off v gå av
get to v komme til
gift gave
gift shop gavebutikk
girl jente
girlfriend kjæreste
give v gi
glacier bre
glass (drinking) glass
glasses (optical) briller
go v gå
go away v gå vekk
go out v gå ut
gold gull
golf golf
golf club golfkølle
golf course golfbane
golf tournament
  golfturnering

good god
good afternoon god dag
good evening god aften
good morning god morgen
good night god natt
goodbye adjø
gram gram
grandchild barnebarn
gray grå
green grønn
greeting hilsen
grocery store
   dagligvarebutikk
ground floor første etasje
guesthouse pensjonat
guide guide
guide dog førerhund
gym trimrom

H

hair hår
hair salon frisørsalong
hairbrush hårbørste
haircut klipp
hairdresser frisør
hairspray hårlakk
halal halal
half halv
handbag håndveske
handicapped
   handikappet
hard hard
hat hatt

have v ha
head hode
headache hodepine
health food store
   helsekostbutikk
health insurance
   sykeforsikring
hearing impaired
   hørselshemmet
heart hjerte
heart condition
   hjertesykdom
heat varme
heater varmeovn
heavy tung
heel hæl
hello hallo
helmet hjelm
help n hjelp; v
   (assist) hjelpe;
   (oneself) ta selv
here her
high høy
highchair babystol
highway motorvei
hill høyde
hire n utleie; v leie
hold on v (phone) vente
   litt
holiday helligdag;
   [BE] ferie
horse hest
hospital sykehus

hot varm
hotel hotell
hour time
house hus
how hvordan
how far hvor langt
how long hvor lenge
how late hvor sent
how many hvor mange
how much hvor mye
hungry sulten
hurry n hastverk
hurt v gjøre vondt
husband ektemann

I

I jeg
ibuprofen ibuprofen
icy kaldt
identification
  legitimasjon
ill [BE] syk
important viktig
impressive imponerende
in i
include v inkludere
indoor pool innendørs
  svømmebasseng
inexpensive rimelig
information informasjon
information desk
  informasjonsskranke
insect insekt

insect bite insektstikk
insect repellent
  insektmiddel
insert v sette inn
inside inni
instant messenger
  lynmelder
insurance forsikring
insurance claim
  forsikringskrav
interesting interessant
international
  internasjonal
internet internett
internet cafe
  internettkafé
interpreter tolk
intersection veikryss
introduce v (person)
  presentere
iron (clothing) strykejern

J

jacket jakke
jazz jazz
jeans olabukse
jet-ski vannscooter
jeweler gullsmed
jewelry smykker
join v (go with
  somebody) bli med
just (only) bare

K

keep v beholde
key nøkkel
key card nøkkelkort
kiddie pool plaskebasseng
kilo kilo
kilometer kilometer
kiss v kysse
knife kniv
know v (something) vite;
(somebody) kjenne
kosher koscher
krone (Norwegian currency) krone

L

lace knipling
lactose intolerant laktoseintolerant
lake innsjø
language språk
large stor
last sist
late sen
later senere
launderette [BE] selvbetjeningsvaskeri
laundromat selvbetjeningsvaskeri
laundry (place) vaskeri; (clothes) vask
laundry facilities vaskemuligheter

lawyer advokat
leather lær
leave v (depart) dra; (deposit) legge igjen
leave alone v la være i fred
left (direction) venstre; (remaining) igjen
lens (for glasses) glass
less mindre
lesson time
letter brev
library bibliotek
life boat livbåt
life jacket flytevest
lifeguard badevakt
lift [BE] (elevator) heis
lift pass heiskort
light adj (weight) lett; adj (color) lys; n lys
light bulb lyspære
lighter lighter
like v like
line linje
linen (cloth) lin
liquor store vinmonopol
liter liter
little (some) litt
live v (exist) leve; (reside) bo
live music levende musikk
loafers mokkasiner
local lokal
lock lås

log in v logge seg inn
log off v logge seg av
log on v logge seg på
long lang
look n titt; v se
lose v miste
loud (voice) høy
love v elske
low lav
luggage bagasje
luggage cart bagasjetralle
luggage locker
  oppbevaringsboks
luggage trolley
  [BE] bagasjetralle
lunch lunsj

M

machine maskin
machine washable
  maskinvaskbar
magazine blad
magnificent storslagen
mail post
mailbox postkasse
make v lage
make up (a prescription)
  [BE] v gjøre i stand
mall kjøpesenter
man mann;
  (gentleman) herre
manager (shop) butikksjef
manicure manikyr

many mange
map kart
market marked
married gift
mass (church) messe
match (matchstick)
  fyrstikk; (sport) kamp
massage massasje
may (can) kunne
meal måltid
mean v bety
measuring cup målebeger
measuring spoon
  måleskje
medication legemiddel
medium mellomstor
meet v møtes
meeting møte
meeting room møterom
memory card minnebrikke
mend v lappe
menstrual cramps
  menstruasjonssmerter
menu meny
message beskjed
meter meter
microwave mikrobølgeovn
midday [BE] middag
midnight midnatt
mileage kjørelengde
minute minutt
miss v mangle
missing savnet

mistake feil
mobile (phone) mobil
moment øyeblikk
money penger
month måned
mop mopp
moped moped
more mer
morning morgen
mosque moské
motion sickness reisesyke
motorcycle motorsykkel
motorboat motorbåt
motorway [BE] motorvei
mountain fjell
mouth munn
move v flytte
movie film
movie theater kino
much mye
mug v overfalle
mugging overfall
museum museum
music musikk
must (have to) måtte

N

nail (human) negl
nail file neglefil
nail salon neglesalong
name navn
napkin serviett

nature preserve
  nasjonalpark
nauseous uvel
near nær
nearby i nærheten
necklace halskjede
need v trenge
new ny
newspaper avis
next neste
next to ved siden av
night natt
nightclub nattklubb
no nei; (not anything) ikke
  noe
no one ingen
non-alcoholic alkoholfri
non-carbonated kullsyrefri
non-smoking (area) for
  ikke-røykere
noon middag
north nord
Norway Norge
Norwegian n nordmann;
  adj norsk
not ikke
nothing ingenting
notify v underrette
novice nybegynner
now nå
number (shoes) nummer;
  (counting) tall
nurse sykepleier

O

off av
off-licence [BE]
  vinmonopol
office kontor
office hours kontortid
old gammel
on på
once én gang
one en
one-way ticket
  enveisbillett
only bare
open v åpne; adj åpen
opera opera
opposite midt imot
optician optiker
order v (meal) bestille
other andre
outdoor pool utendørs
  svømmebasseng
outlet (electric)
  stikkontakt
overlook utsikt
overnight natten over

P

p.m. (afternoon) om
  ettermiddagen;
  (evening) om kvelden
pacifier (baby's)
  narresmokk
pack v pakke

package pakke
paddling pool [BE]
  plaskebasseng
pain smerte
pajamas pyjamas
palace slott
pants langbukse
panty hose strømpebukse
paper papir
paper towel
  husholdningspapir
paracetamol
  [BE] paracetamol
park n park; v parkere
parking lot
  parkeringsplass
part time deltid
pass through v være på
  gjennomreise
passport pass
passport control
  passkontroll
password passord
pastry bakverk
pastry shop konditori
path sti
pay v betale
peak topp
pearl perle
pediatrician barnelege
pedicure fotpleie
pen penn
penicillin penicillin

pensioner pensjonist
per day per dag
per hour per time
per kilometer per kilometer
per night per natt
per week per uke
perfume parfyme
period (menstruation) menstruasjon
permit v tillate
petrol [BE] bensin
petrol station [BE] bensinstasjon
pewter tinn
pharmacy apotek
phone telefon
phone call telefonsamtale
phone card telefonkort
phone number telefonnummer
photo foto
photocopy fotokopi
photograph fotografi
pick up v (person) hente
picnic picnic
picnic area turområde
piece stykke
pill pille; (contraceptive) p-pille
pillow pute
pink rosa

piste [BE] løype
piste map [BE] løypekart
place n (location) sted; (in hostel) plass
plaster [BE] (bandage) plaster
plastic wrap plastfolie
plate tallerken; (dessert) asjett
platform [BE] (station) perrong
play n (theatre) stykke; v spille
playground lekeplass
playing card spillkort
playpen lekegrind
please adv vær så snill
plunger klosettpumpe
pocket lomme
point v peke
point of interest severdighet
poles (ski) staver
police politi
police report politirapport
police station politistasjon
pond dam
pop music popmusikk
portion porsjon
possible mulig
post (mail) [BE] post
postage stamp frimerke
postbox [BE] postkasse

postcard postkort
post office postkontor
pot gryte
pound (British
  currency) pund
pregnant gravid
premium (gas) super
prepaid calling
  time ringetid
prescription resept
press v (iron) presse
pressure trykk
price pris
print v skrive ut; n
  (photo) kopi
problem problem
pronounce v uttale
pronunciation uttale
pull v trekke
purple fiolett
push v (open) skyve
pushchair [BE] gåstol
put v sette
put through sette over

Q

question spørsmål
quick rask
quickly øyeblikkelig
quiet rolig

R

racecourse [BE] travbane

racetrack travbane
racket (sport) racket
railway station [BE]
  jernbanestasjon
rain n regn; v regne
raincoat regnfrakk
rainy regnfull
rap (music) rap
rape voldtekt
rash utslett
rate (exchange) kurs
razor barberhøvel
razor blade barberblad
reach v nå
ready klar
real (genuine) ekte
receipt kvittering
receive v motta
recommend v anbefale
red rød
refrigerator kjøleskap
region område
regular (fuel)
  normalbensin
reindeer skin
  reinsdyrskinn
relationship forhold
rent v leie
rental car leiebil
repair v reparere
repeat gjenta
report n rapport; v
  (a crime) anmelde

reservation bestilling
reserve v bestille
restaurant restaurant
restroom toalett
retired (from work) pensjonert
return v (**come back**) komme tilbake; (**give back**) levere tilbake
return ticket [BE] tur-returbillett
right (correct) rett; (**direction**) høyre
ring (jewelry) ring
river elv
road vei
road map veikart
road sign trafikkskilt
rob rane
romantic romantisk
room rom
room service romservice
round (golf) runde
round-trip ticket tur-returbillett
route rute
rowboat robåt
rubbish [BE] søppel
rubbish bag [BE] søppelsekk
ruin ruin

S

safe adj (**free from danger**) trygg; n safe
sandals sandaler
sanitary napkin sanitetsbind
saucer skål
sauna badstue
save (computer) lagre
scarf skjerf
schedule (transport) rutetabell
scissors saks
sea sjø
sealskin slippers selskinnstøfler
seat plass
see v (**watch**) se; (**meet**) treffe; (**examine**) undersøke
sell v selge
seminar seminar
send v sende
senior citizen pensjonist
separately hver for seg
separated separert
sentence setning
serve v servere
service service; (**church**) gudstjeneste
shampoo sjampo
should burde

sheet laken
ship n skip; v sende
shirt skjorte
shoe store skobutikk
shoes sko
shop butikk
shopping area handlestrøk
shopping centre [BE]
  butikksenter
shopping mall
  butikksenter
shopping trolley [BE]
  handlevogn
short kort
shorts shorts
show v vise
shower dusj
shrine helligdom
sick (ill) syk
side side
side effect bivirkning
sightseeing sightseeing
sightseeing tour
  sightseeingtur
sign v undertegne
silk silke
silver sølv
single (unmarried) ugift
single room enkeltrom
single ticket [BE]
  enveisbillett
size (clothes) størrelse;
  (shoes) nummer

ski v gå på ski
skis ski
ski lift skiheis
skirt skjørt
slice skive
slippers tøfler
slow langsom
slowly langsomt
small liten
smoke røyke
smoking (area) for røykere
sneakers turnsko
snorkeling equipment
  snorkleutstyr
snow n snø; v snø
snowboard snøbrett
snowshoes truger
soap såpe
soccer fotball
soccer game fotballkamp
sock sokk
someone noen
something noe
somewhere et eller annet
  sted
soon snart
sore throat sår hals
sorry v beklage
south sør
souvenir suvenir
souvenir store
  suvenirbutikk
spa spa

speak v snakke
speciality spesialitet
spoon skje
sports idrett
sports massage
  idrettsmassasje
sprained forstuet
square plass
stadium stadion
stairs trapp
stamp v stemple;
  n (postage) frimerke
start v starte
station stasjon
stay v (remain) bli;
  (reside) bo
steal v stjele
steep bratt
sterling silver sterlingsølv
stocking strømpe
stolen stjålet
stomach mage
stomachache
  magesmerte
stop n (place)
  holdeplass; v stoppe
store (shop) butikk
store directory
  butikkguide
stove komfyr
straight ahead rett frem
strange underlig

stream bekk
street gate
stroller gåstol
student student
study v studere
stunning overveldende
style v (hair) style
subway T-bane
subway station
  T-banestasjon
suit n (man's) dress;
  (woman's) drakt
suitable passende
suitcase koffert
sun sol
sunburn solforbrenning
sunglasses solbriller
sunscreen solkrem
sunstroke solstikk
super (gas) superbensin
supermarket
  supermarked
surfboard surfebrett
swallow v svelge
sweater genser
swelling hevelse
swim v svømme
swimming pool
  svømmebasseng
swimming trunks
  badebukse
swimsuit badedrakt

symbol tegn
synagogue synagoge

T

table bord
tablet (medical) tablett
take v ta
tampon tampong
taste v smake
tax skatt
taxi drosje
taxi rank [BE] drosjeholdeplass
taxi stand drosjeholdeplass
team lag
teaspoon teskje
tell v si
temple (religious) tempel
tennis tennis
tennis court tennisbane
tennis match tenniskamp
tent telt
terminal (airport) terminal
terrible forferdelig
text n tekst; v (message) tekste
than enn
thank v takke
theft tyveri
there (place) der; (direction) dit

these disse
thief tyv
thing ting
think v (believe) tro
this denne; dette
those de
throat hals
ticket billett
ticket office billettluke
tights [BE] strømpebukse
time (period) tid; (occasion) gang
timetable [BE] rutetabell
tissue papirlommetørkle
to (direction) til; (time) på
tobacco tobakk
tobacconist tobakkshandel
today i dag
toilet [BE] toalett
toilet paper toalettpapir
tomorrow i morgen
tonight i kveld
too for
tooth tann
toothache tannpine
toothbrush tannbørste
toothpaste tannpasta
tour tur
tourist office turistkontor
towel håndkle
town by

town map bykart
town square torg
toy leketøy
toy store leketøysbutikk
track (railway) spor
traditional tradisjonell
traffic light trafikklys
trail løype
trail map løypekart
train tog
train schedule togtabell
train station
  jernbanestasjon
tram trikk
translate v oversette
trash søppel
travel v reise
travel agency reisebyrå
travel guide
  reisehåndbok
travel sickness reisesyke
traveler's check
  reisesjekk
trim (hair) stuss
trip tur
troll troll
trousers [BE] langbukse
try on v prøve
T-shirt T-skjorte
turn off (device) skru av
turn on (device) skru på

TV TV
type v (computer) skrive
typically typisk

U

ugly stygg
umbrella paraply
underground [BE]
  n T-bane
underground station [BE]
  T-banestasjon
undershirt trøye
understand v forstå
unleaded blyfri
until til
upset stomach
  urolig mage
use n bruk; v bruke
username brukernavn

V

vacation ferie
vacuum cleaner
  støvsuger
vaginal infection
  underlivsbetennelse
valley dal
value verdi
VAT [BE] moms
vegetarian vegetarianer
very meget

viking ship vikingskip
visit *n* besøk; *v* **(a person)** besøke
visiting hours besøkstid
visually impaired synshemmet
volleyball game volleyballkamp
vomit *v* kaste opp

W

wait *v* vente
waiter servitør
waitress servitør
wake *v* vekke
wake-up call vekking
walk *v* **(go)** gå; **(stroll)** spasere
wallet lommebok
want *v* ville
warm *adj* varm; *v* varme
wash *v* vaske
washable vaskbar
washing mashine vaskemaskin
watch klokke
water vann
waterfall foss
water skis vannski
weather vær
weather forecast værutsikter
week uke
weekend helg
welcome velkommen
west vest
what hva
wheelchair rullestol
wheelchair ramp rullestolsrampe
when når
where hvor
which hvilken
white hvit
who hvem
whole hel
widowed (man) enkemann; **(woman)** enke
wife kone
window vindu
window seat vindusplass
windsurfer seilbrett
wine list vinkart
wireless internet trådløst internett
with med
withdraw *v* **(from account)** ta ut
without uten
woman kvinne
wooden figurine trefigur
wool ull

work *v* **(toil)** arbeide;
  (function) virke
wrap up *v* pakke inn
write *v* skrive
wrong i veien

Y

year år
yellow gul
yes ja
yesterday i går
you du
youth hostel vandrerhjem

Z

zoo dyrehage

NORWEGIAN–ENGLISH

A

adapter adapter
adjø goodbye
adresse address
advokat lawyer
akkurat nå right now
akupunktur acupuncture
alkoholfri non-alcoholic
allergisk allergic
allergisk reaksjon
  allergic reaction
alt all
aluminiumsfolie
  aluminum foil
amerikaner n American
amerikansk adj American
anbefale v recommend
andre other
ankomst arrival
anmelde v report (a theft)
annen rute alternate route
annullere v cancel
ansikt face
ansiktsbehandling facial
antibiotikum antibiotic
antikvitet antique
antikvitetshandel
  antiques store
antiseptisk salve
  antiseptic cream

aperitiff aperitif
apotek pharmacy [chemist BE]
arbeide v work
armbånd bracelet
aromaterapi aromatherapy
asjett plate (dessert)
aspirin aspirin
astma asthma
automatisk automatic
av off
avgang departure
avis newspaper
avtale appointment

B

baby baby
babystol highchair
bad bathroom
badebukse swimming trunks
badedrakt swimsuit
badevakt lifeguard
badstue sauna
bagasje luggage [baggage
  BE]
bagasjemottak baggage
  claim
bagasjetralle luggage cart
  [trolley BE]
bak behind
bakeri bakery

bakverk pastry
bandasje bandage
bank bank (finance)
bar *n* bar (place)
barberblad razor blade
barberhøvel razor
bare just; only
barn child
barnebarn grandchild
barnelege pediatrician
barnemeny children's menu
barneporsjon children's portion
barnesete car seat
barnevakt babysitter
basketball basketball
batteri battery
be om *v* ask for
begivenhet event
begynner beginner
beholde *v* keep
behå bra
beige beige
bekk stream
beklage *v* be sorry
bekrefte *v* confirm
belte belt
bensin gas [petrol BE] (car)
bensinstasjon gas [petrol BE] station
beskjed message
best best

bestille *v* order (meal); reserve
bestilling reservation
besøk *n* visit
besøke *v* visit (someone)
besøkstid visiting hours
betale *v* pay
bety *v* mean
bevegelseshemmet disabled
bibliotek library
bikini bikini
bil car
billett ticket
billettluke ticket office
billig cheap
bilutleie car rental [hire BE]
bivirkning side effect
blad magazine
bleie diaper
bli *v* stay (remain)
bli med *v* join (someone)
blind blind
blod blood
blodfattig anemic [anaemic BE]
blodtrykk blood pressure
blomst flower
bluse blouse
blyfri unleaded
blø *v* bleed
blå blue
bo live (reside); stay (reside)

bok book
bokhandel bookstore
boks can (container)
boksåpner can opener
bolle bowl
bomull cotton
bondegård farm
bord table
botanisk hage botanical gardens
bra fine (OK)
brann fire (disaster)
branndør fire door
bratt steep
bre glacier
brev letter
briller glasses
britisk British
bro bridge
brosje brooch
bruk n use
bruke v use
brukernavn username
brukket broken (bone)
brun brown
bryst chest
burde should
buss bus
bussholdeplass bus stop
busstasjon bus station
butikk store [shop BE]
butikkguide store directory
butikksenter shopping mall [centre BE]
butikksjef manager (shop)
by n city; town
bykart town map
bytte v change (transportation)
bytte på v change (baby)
bære v carry
bærepose bag (carrier)
båt boat

C

campe v camp
camping camping
campingplass campsite

D

dag day
dagligvarebutikk grocery store
dal valley
dam pond
danse v dance
dansk Danish
datamaskin computer
delikatesseforretning delicatessen
deltid part time
denne this
deodorant deodorant
depositum deposit (down payment)
der there (place)

dette this
diabetiker diabetic
diamant diamond
diarré diarrhea
die breastfeed
diesel diesel
digital digital
digitalkamera digital camera
digitalt bilde digital photo
diskotek dance club
disse these
dit there (direction)
dobbel double
dobbeltrom double room
dobbeltseng double bed
dollar dollar
domkirke cathedral
dongeri denim
dra v leave (depart)
drakt suit (woman's)
dress suit (man's)
drikk n drink
drikke v drink
drikkekart drink menu
drosje taxi
drosjeholdeplass taxi stand [rank BE]
dråpe drop (liquid)
du you
dukke doll
dusj shower
dykke v dive
dykkeutstyr diving equipment
dyp adj deep
dyr adj expensive
dyrehage zoo
dør door
døv deaf

E

e-billett e-ticket
ekspert expert
ekspress express
ekspresspost express mail
ekstra extra
ekstra stor extra large
ekte real (genuine)
ektemann husband
ekthetssertifikat certificate of authenticity
elske v love
elv river
en a (common nouns); one
endre v change
engangshøvel disposable razor
engangskamera disposable camera
engelsk English
engelsktalende English-speaking
enke widowed (woman)
enkeltrom single room
enkemann widowed (man)
enn than

enveisbillett one-way [single BE] ticket
e-post e-mail
e-postadresse e-mail addess
erfaren experienced
et a (neuter nouns)
et eller annet sted somewhere
et øyeblikk hold on (phone)
etasje floor
etter after
ettermiddag afternoon

F

faks n fax
fakse v fax
faksnummer fax number
familie family
farge color
fat dish
feber fever
feiekost broom
feil mistake
ferge ferry
ferie vacation [holiday BE]
fersk fresh
film movie
fiolett purple
fjell mountain
fjord fjord
flaske bottle

flaskeåpner bottle opener
fluktstol deck chair
fly flight
flyplass airport
flyselskap airline
flytevest life jacket
flytte v move
folkemusikk folk music
fontene fountain
for for; too
for røykere smoking (area)
forferdelig terrible
forhold relationship
forkjølelse cold (illness)
fornøyelsespark amusement park
forretning business
forretningssenter business center
forrett appetizer
forsikring insurance
forsikringskrav insurance claim
forsinkelse delay
forsinket delayed
forstoppelse constipation
forstuet sprained
forstå v understand
fortolle v declare (customs)
foss waterfall
fot foot
fotball soccer [football BE]

fotballkamp soccer [football BE] game
foto photo
fotokopi photocopy
fotpleie pedicure
fra from
frakk coat (man's)
fri free
frimerke stamp (postage)
frisør hairdresser
frisørsalong hair salon
frokost breakfast
fryser freezer
full full
fylle v fill up
fylle ut v fill out
fyrstikk match (matchstick)
fødselsdag birthday
før before
førerhund guide dog
førerkort driver's license [driving licence BE]
første etasje ground floor
første klasse first class
få motorstopp v break down (car)
få tak i v get (find)

G

gaffel fork
gammel old
gang time (occasion)
gate street

gave gift
gavebutikk gift shop
gebiss denture
gebyr fee
genser sweater
gi v give
gift adj married
gir n speed (cycle)
gjenta v repeat
gjøre v do
gjøre i stand v make up (prepare)
gjøre vondt v hurt
glass glass (drinking)
glass lens (for glasses)
god good
god aften good evening
god dag good afternoon
god morgen good morning
god natt good night
godter candy
golf golf
golfbane golf course
golfkølle golf club
golfturnering golf tournament
gram gram
gravere v engrave
gravid pregnant
gryte pot
grå gray
grønn green
gudstjeneste service (church)

guide guide
gul *adj* yellow
gull *n* gold
gullsmed jeweler
gult gull yellow gold
gutt boy
gå *v* go; walk
gå av *v* get off
gå inn *v* enter
gå på ski *v* ski
gå seg bort *v* get lost
gå ut *v* go out
gå vekk go away
gåstol stroller [pushchair, buggy BE]
gått i stykker broken (out of order)

H

ha *v* have
ha det travelt *v* be in a hurry
ha gått seg bort *v* be lost
hage garden
halal halal
hallo hello
hals throat
halskjede necklace
halv half
halvtime half an hour
handikappet handicapped
handlekurv basket (shopping)

handlestrøk shopping area
handlevogn shopping cart [trolley BE]
hans his
hard hard
haste *v* to be urgent
hatt hat
heis elevator [lift BE]
heiskort lift pass
hel whole
helg weekend
helligdag holiday
helligdom shrine
helsekostbutikk health food store
heltid full time
hennes her
hente *v* pick up (person)
her here
herre man (gentleman)
herrefrisør barber
hest horse
hevelse swelling
hilsen greeting
hjelm helmet
hjelp *n* help
hjelpe *v* help
hjerte heart
hjertesykdom heart condition
hjørne corner
hode head
hodepine headache

holde rundt hug
holdeplass stop (place)
hoste v cough
hotell hotel
hule n cave
hullsleiv spatula
hund dog
hurtig fast
hus house
husholdningspapir paper towel
hva what
hvem who
hver for oss separately
hvilken which
hvit white
hvitt gull white gold
hvor where
hvor langt how far
hvor lenge how long
hvor mange how many
hvor mye how much
hvor sent how late
hvordan how
hæl heel
hørselshemmet hearing impaired
høy high (tall); loud (voice)
høyde hill
høyre right (direction)
håndbagasje carry-on (luggage)
håndkle towel

håndveske handbag
hår hair
hårbalsam conditioner (hair)
hårbørste hairbrush
hårlakk hair spray

I

i in
i dag today
i går yesterday
i kveld tonight
i morgen tomorrow
i nærheten nearby
i veien wrong
ibuprofen ibuprofen (pharmaceutical)
idrett sports
idrettsmassasje sports massage
igjen left (remaining)
ikke not
ikke noe no (not anything)
ild fire (open)
imponerende impressive
informasjon information
informasjonsskranke information desk
ingen no one
ingenting nothing
inkludere v include
inkludert included
inneholde v contain

innendørs svømmebasseng indoor pool

innenlands domestic

inngangsbillett admission (price)

inngangspenger cover charge

inni inside

innkvartering accommodations [accomodation BE]

innsjekkingsskranke check-in

innsjø lake

insekt insect, bug

insektmiddel insect repellent

insektstikk insect bite

interessant interesting

interessert interested

internasjonal international

internett internet

internettkafé internet cafe

J

ja yes

jakke jacket

jazz jazz

jeg I

jente girl

jernbanestasjon train [railway BE] station

jorde field

K

kafé cafe

kald cold

kaldt icy

kam comb

kamera camera

kamp game; match (sport)

karaffel carafe

kart map

kartong carton

kasse cash desk

kaste opp v vomit

kelner waiter

kilo kilo

kilometer kilometer [kilometre BE]

kino movie theater [cinema BE]

kirke church

kjedelig boring

kjemisk toalett chemical toilet

kjenne v know (somebody)

kjole dress

kjæreste boyfriend; girlfriend

kjøleskap refrigerator

kjøpe buy

kjøpesenter mall

kjøre *v* drive
kjørelengde mileage
klar ready
klassisk musikk classical music
klesbutikk clothing store
kleskode dress code
klimaanlegg air conditioning
klipp haircut
klippe *n* cliff; *v* cut (with scissors)
klokke watch
klosettpumpe plunger
knipling lace
kniv knife
kobber copper
koffert suitcase
kokemuligheter cooking facilities
kollega colleague
komfyr stove
komme *v* come
komme frem *v* arrive
komme til *v* get to
komme tilbake *v* return (come back)
konditori pastry shop
kondom condom
kone wife
konferanse conference
konferansesenter convention hall

konsert concert
kontaktlinse contact lens
kontaktlinsevæske contact lens solution
kontanter cash
konto account
kontor office
kontortid office hours
kontroll control
kopi print (photo)
kopp cup
korketrekker corkscrew
kort *n* card; *adj* short
koscher kosher
koste *v* cost
kredittkort credit card
krone krone (Norwegian currency)
krystall crystal
kullsyrefri non-carbonated [still BE] (drink)
kunne can; may
kurs rate (of exchange)
kveld evening
kvinne woman
kvittering receipt
kysse *v* kiss
kåpe coat (woman's)

L

la oss let's
la være i fred *v* leave alone
lag team

lage *v* make

lagre *v* save (computer)

laken sheet

laktoseintolerant lactose intolerant

land country; countryside

landekode country code

lang long

langbukser pants [trousers BE]

langsom slow

langsomt slowly

langt far

lappe *v* mend

lav low

lavhælt flat (shoe)

leddgikt arthritis

lege doctor

legemiddel medication

legge igjen *v* leave (deposit)

legitimasjon identification

leie *v* hire; rent

leiebil rental car

leilighet apartment

lekegrind playpen

lekeplass playground

leketøy toy

leketøysbutikk toy store

lett easy; light (weight)

leve *v* live

levende musikk live music

levere tilbake *v* return (give back)

lighter lighter

like *v* like

lin linen (cloth)

linje line (transport); extension (phone)

liten small

liter liter

litt little; some (with singular nouns)

livbåt life boat

logge seg av log off

logge seg inn log in

logge seg på log on

lokal local

lomme pocket

lommebok wallet

lunsj lunch

lusekofte cardigan (Norwegian)

lynmelder instant messenger

lys *n* light; *adj* light (color)

lysestake candlestick

lyspære light bulb

lær leather

løse inn *v* cash

løype trail [piste BE]

løypekart trail map [piste map BE]

lås lock

låse seg ute *v* lock oneself out

M

mage stomach
magesmerte stomachache
mange many
mangle v miss
manikyr manicure
mann man
marked market
maskin machine
maskinvaskbar machine washable
massasje massage
mat food
mate v feed
med with
meget very
melkeprodukter dairy
mellomstor medium
men but
menstruasjon period (monthly)
menstruasjonssmerter menstrual cramps
meny menu
mer more
messe mass (church)
meter meter
middag dinner (meal); noon [midday BE]
midnatt midnight
midt imot opposite
midtgang aisle

mikrobølgeovn microwave
mindre less
minibank ATM
minnebrikke memory card
minutt minute
miste v lose
mobil cell [mobile BE] phone
mokkasiner loafers
moms sales tax [VAT BE]
monter display case
moped moped
mopp mop
morgen morning
morsmelkerstatning formula
moské mosque
motorbåt motorboat
motorsykkel motorcycle
motorvei highway [motorway BE]
motta v receive
mulig possible
munn mouth
museum museum
musikk music
mye much
mynt coin
mørk dark
møte meeting
møterom meeting room
møtes v meet
målebeger measuring cup

måleskje measuring spoon
måltid meal
måned month
måtte v must (have to)

N

narresmokk pacifier [dummy BE] (baby's)
nasjonalpark nature preserve
natt night
natten over overnight
nattklubb nightclub
navn name
ned down
negl nail (human)
neglefil nail file
neglesalong nail salon
nei no
neste next
noe any; anything; something
noen anyone; some (with plural nouns); someone
nord north
Norge Norway
normalbensin regular (fuel)
norsk Norwegian
nummer number (counting); size (shoes)
ny new

nybegynner novice
nyte v enjoy
nær near
nærmeste nearest
nødutgang emergency exit
nøkkel key
nøkkelkort key card
nå adv now; v reach
når when

O

olabukser jeans
om ettermiddagen p.m. (afternoon)
om kvelden p.m. (evening)
om morgenen a.m.
ombordstigning boarding
ombordstigningskort boarding pass
område area; region
opera opera
oppbevaringsboks luggage locker
opptatt busy
oppvaskmaskin dishwasher
oppvaskmiddel dish detergent [washing-up liquid BE]
optiker optician
ordbok dictionary
ostehøvel cheese slicer
overfall attack; mugging

overfalle v mug
oversette v translate
overvektig bagasje excess luggage
overveldende stunning

P

p-pille pill (contraceptive)
pakke package [parcel BE]; v pack
pakke inn v wrap up
palass palace
papir paper
papirkluter baby wipes
papirkopi av et digitalt bilde digital print
papirlommetørkle tissue
paracetamol acetaminophen [paracetamol BE]
paraply umbrella
parfyme perfume
parfymeri perfumery
park n park
parkere v park
parkeringsplass parking lot [car park BE]
pass passport
passe v fit
passende suitable
passkontroll passport control

passord password
peke v point
penger money
penicillin penicillin
penn pen
pensjonat guesthouse
pensjonert retired (from work)
pensjonist senior citizen
per dag per day
per kilometer per kilometer [kilometre BE]
per natt per night
per time per hour
per uke per week
perle pearl
perrong platform [BE] (station)
picnic picnic
pille pill
plage v bother
plaskebasseng kiddie [paddling BE] pool
plass place (hostel); seat; square
plaster bandage [plaster BE]
plastfolie plastic wrap [cling film BE]
plombe filling (tooth)
politi police
politirapport police report

politistasjon police station

popmusikk pop music

porsjon portion

post mail [post BE]

postkasse mailbox [postbox BE]

postkontor post office

postkort postcard

praktfull amazing

presentere v introduce (person)

presse v press (iron)

pris price

problem problem

protestantisk Protestant

prøve v try on

prøverom fitting room

pund pound (money)

puste v breathe

pute pillow

pyjamas pajamas

på on (place); to (time)

R

rabatt discount

racket racket (sport)

rane rob

rap rap (music)

rapport report

rask quick

regn n rain

regne v rain

regnfrakk raincoat

regnfull rainy

regning n check [bill BE] (restaurant)

reinsdyrskinn reindeer skin

reise v travel

reisebyrå travel agency

reisehåndbok travel guide

reisesjekk traveler's check [cheque BE]

reisesyke motion sickness

ren clean

rengjøringsmidler cleaning supplies

renseri dry cleaner

reparere v fix; repair

resept prescription

restaurant restaurant

retning direction

retningsnummer area code

rett dish (food); right (correct)

rett frem straight ahead

rimelig inexpensive

ring n ring (jewelry)

ringe v call (phone)

ringetid prepaid calling time

robåt rowboat

rolig quiet

rom room

romantisk romantic
romservice room service
rosa pink
ruin *n* ruin
rullestol wheelchair
rullestolsrampe
  wheelchair ramp
rulletrapp escalator
runde round (golf)
rundt around (nearby)
rute route
rutetabell schedule
  [timetable BE]
  (transportation)
rygg back (body part)
ryggsekk backpack
rød red
røyke *v* smoke
røykfri non-smoking (area)

S

safe *n* safe; *adj* trygg
saks scissors
salve cream
  (pharmaceutical)
samtale call (phone)
sandaler sandals
sanitetsbind sanitary
  napkin [towel BE]
savnet missing
se *v* look; see
seilbrett windsurfer
selge *v* sell

selvbetjeningsvaskeri
  laundromat [launderette
  BE]
seminar seminar
sen late
sende *v* send; ship
sende e-post *v* e-mail
senere later
seng bed
sentrum downtown area
separert separated
servere *v* serve
service service
serviett napkin
servitør waiter, waitress
sete ved midtgangen aisle
  seat
setning sentence
sette *v* put
sette inn *v* insert
sette over *v* put through
severdighet point of interest
shorts shorts
si *v* tell
side side
sigar cigar
sigarett cigarette
sightseeing sightseeing
sightseeingtur
  sightseeing tour
silke silk
sist last
sjampo shampoo

sjekk *n* check [cheque BE]
sjekke e-post *v* check e-mail
sjekke inn check in (airport)
sjekke ut check out
sjø sea
skade *v* damage
skatt tax
ski skis
skiheis ski lift
skilt divorced
skip ship
skitrekk drag lift
skitten dirty
skive slice
skje spoon
skjema form (document)
skjerf scarf
skjorte shirt
skjørt skirt
sko shoes
skobutikk shoe store
skog forest
skrive *v* write; type (computer)
skrive ut *v* print
skru av *v* turn off (device)
skru på *v* turn on (device)
skyve *v* push (open)
skål saucer; cheers (a toast)
slagsted battleground
sleiv spatula

slett *v* clear (ATM)
slette *v* delete (computer)
slott castle
slutt *n* end
slutte *v* end
smake *v* taste
smakløs bland
smerte pain
smykker jewelry
snakke *v* speak
snart soon
snorkleutstyr snorkeling equipment
snø *n/v* snow
snøbrett snowboard
sokk sock
sol sun
solbriller sunglasses
solforbrenning sunburn
solkrem sunscreen
solstikk sunstroke
sommer summer
spa spa
spasere *v* walk (stroll)
spesialitet speciality
spille *v* play
spille på hester *v* place a bet
spillehall arcade
spillkort playing card
spise *v* eat
spisekart menu (printed)
spor track (railway)

springvann tap water
sprinkelseng crib
[child's cot BE]
språk language
spørre v ask
spørsmål question
stadion stadium
starte v start
stasjon station
staver poles (ski)
sted place
stekepanne frying pan
stemple stamp
stenge v close
stengt closed
sterlingsølv sterling silver
sti path
stikkontakt outlet (electric)
[socket BE]
stjele v steal
stjålet stolen
stol chair
stolheis chair lift
stoppe v stop
stor big; large
stormagasin department
store
storslagen magnificent
strand beach
strykejern iron (clothing)
strømpe stocking
strømpebukse panty hose
[tights BE]
strømuttak electrical outlet

student student
studere v study
stuss trim (hair)
stygg ugly
stykke piece; play (theater)
style v style (hair)
større bigger
størrelse size (clothes)
støvel boot
støvsuger vacuum cleaner
sulten hungry
super premium; super
(gasoline)
supermarked
supermarket
surfebrett surfboard
surstoffbehandling
oxygen treatment
suvenir souvenir
suvenirbutikk souvenir store
svart black
svelge v swallow
svensk Swedish
Sverige Sweden
svimmel dizzy
svømme v swim
svømmebasseng
swimming pool
syk sick [ill BE]
sykebil ambulance
sykeforsikring
health insurance
sykehus hospital
sykepleier nurse

sykkel bicycle
sykkelløp cycling race
sykkelsti bike route
sykling cycling
synagoge synagogue
synshemmet visually impaired
sølv silver
søppel trash [rubbish BE]
søppelsekk garbage [rubbish BE] bag
sør south
søt cute
søvnighet drowsiness
såpe soap
sår hals sore throat

T

T-bane subway [underground BE]
T-banestasjon subway [underground BE] station
T-skjorte T-shirt
ta v take
ta med v bring (something)
ta med seg v take away (carry)
ta selv v help (oneself)
ta ut v withdraw (from account)
tablett tablet (medical)
takke v thank
tall number (counting)
tallerken plate

tampong tampon
tann tooth
tannlege dentist
tannbørste toothbrush
tannpasta toothpaste
tannpine toothache
taubane cable car
tegn symbol
tekst n text (message)
tekste v text (someone)
telefon phone
telefonkort phone card
telefonnummer phone number
telefonsamtale phone call
telt tent
tempel temple (religion)
tenke på v think about
tennis tennis
tennisbane tennis court
tenniskamp tennis match
terminal terminal (airport)
teskje teaspoon
tid time
til to (direction)
til until (time)
tilbake back (direction)
tilbehør accessories
tillate v permit
tillatt allowed
tiltrekkende attractive
time hour; lesson
ting thing
tinn pewter

titt look
toalett restroom [toilet BE]
toalettpapir toilet paper
tobakk tobacco
tobakkshandel tobacconist's
tog train
togtabell train schedule [timetable BE]
tolk interpreter
toll customs; duty (tax)
tollfri duty-free
tom empty
topp peak
torg town square
tradisjonell traditional
trafikklys traffic light
trafikkskilt road sign
tralle cart (luggage)
trapp stairs
travbane racetrack [race course BE]
treffe v see (meet)
trefigur wooden figurine
trekke v pull
trenge v need
treningsdrakt sweatsuit
trikk tram BE
trimrom gym
tro v think (believe)
truger snowshoes
trygg safe (free from danger)
trykk pressure

trøye undershirt
trådløst internett wireless internet
tung heavy
tur tour; trip
tur-returbillett round-trip [return BE ticket]
turistklasse economy class
turistkontor tourist office
turnsko sneakers
turområde picnic area
tursti walking route
TV TV
typisk typically
tyv thief
tyveri theft
tøfler slippers
tøm v empty
tørr adj dry
tåteflaske baby bottle

U

ugift single (unmarried)
uke week
ull wool
ukentlig adj weekly
ullteppe blanket
ulykke accident
underbukse panties, drawers, shorts
underlig strange
underrette v notify
undersøke v see (examine)

undertegne v sign
ungdomsherberge youth hostel
unge kid
universitet university
unnskyld! sorry!
unnskylde v excuse
urolig mage upset stomach
uten without
utendørs svømmebasseng outdoor pool
utenfor outside
utflukt excursion, trip, outing
utgang exit; gate
utleie hire
utsikt overlook
utsjekking check out
utslett rash
utstyr equipment
uttale v pronounce; n pronunciation
uvel nauseous

V

vakker beautiful
valuta currency
vandrerhjem youth hostel
vann water
vannscooter jet ski
vannski water skis
vanskelig difficult
vare goods

varm hot; warm
varme n heat [heating BE]; v warm
varmeovn heater
vask laundry (clothes)
vaskbar washable
vaske v clean; wash
vaskemaskin washing mashine
vaskemiddel detergent
vaskemuligheter laundry facilities
ved prep at, by, on n firewood
ved siden av next to
vegetarianer vegetarian
vei road
veikart road map
veikryss intersection
vekke v wake
vekking wake-up call
veksle v change (money); exchange
vekslepenger n change (money)
vekslingskontor currency exchange office
vekslingskurs exchange rate
velkommen welcome
venn friend
venstre left
vente v wait
vente på v wait for

verdi value
vest west
vifte fan (appliance)
vikingskip viking ship
viktig important
ville want to
vindu window
vindusplass window seat
vinkart wine list
vinmonopol liquor store
  [off-licence BE]
vinter winter
virke v work (function)
vise v show
visittkort business card
vite v know (something)
voldtekt rape
volleyballkamp volleyball
  game
vondt i brystet chest pain
vær så snill please
vær weather
være v be
værutsikter weather
  forecast

Ø

ørering earring
øreverk earache
øst east
øye eye
øyeblikk moment
øyeblikkelig quickly
øyenbryn eyebrow

øyenskygge eye shadow
øyensverte mascara
øyenvitne eye witness

Å

åpen adj open
åpne v open
åpningstid v business
  hours
år year
årstid season
åtti eighty